Candy _____ My Miracle from God

Jeremiah
29:11
Candy

Candy Kisses
My Miracle from God
JOHN 11:25

A MOM'S JOURNEY IN FAITH

Mary Ellen Sparks

...he that believeth in me,
though he were dead,
yet shall he live;
—John 11:25

Another Quality Book Published By:
LEGACY BOOK PUBLISHING
1883 Lee Road, Winter Park, FL 32789
www.LegacyBookPublishing.com

The cover illustration in pencil is titled "Sarah" from the 'For They Shall Be Comforted series' by Jean Keaton used by permission. Prints of this and other wonderful illustratons are available at: www.keatonprints.com

Candy Kisses My Miracle from God:
A Mom's Journey in Faith

Published by:
LEGACY Book Publishing
1883 Lee Road
Winter Park, Florida 32789
www.LegacyBookPublishing.com

Cover Design by Gabriel H. Vaughn

To God be the Glory!

This book is dedicated to the memory of:
Mom and Dad
Larry Sexton my brother
Dallas Johnson my nephew
and
Sonya Terrell, Candy's special friend

If only I could build a staircase up to heaven . . .

Table of Contents

me find healing for my Candy
Let's join our faith and believe God for a miracle
Mr. Hall's lawnmower repairs
Look at me; I'm riding a bicycle
Want God to talk to you?

Introduction

"*Look out, world, here I come!*" That was probably my first thought when I first came into this world. My name is Candy or *Candy Kisses,* as my Mom calls me. As my journey begins I am eleven years old, soon to be twelve, the following month. Come with me, my Mom, Daddy and big brother Jason on this life-changing journey **as written by my Mom**. This journey, in fact, also includes my town of Odenville and everyone in it. We didn't have to go alone on this journey. The entire town and all my friends and relatives went with us.

This is a journey toward faith that kept me alive; in fact my Mom calls me her "*Miracle from God*" because she says this faith actually brought me back to life after being dead about five minutes.

This journey will sometimes make you cry; sometimes you will laugh, but through it all you will see how we survived. It worked for us and it can work for you. You will see that many people were part of my life story. They all played major roles. God was there the whole time. He found us early in our devastation. God placed so many people in our path to help us.

My whole world changed on that terrible April 1st so many years ago. (No wonder they call it April Fool's Day.) On this journey, I battled three life-threatening illnesses at the same time. Everything was backwards for me. Things that worked for other kids had reverse effects for me. I had things happen to me that hadn't happened before. I really thought it was the end of the world for me and actually sometimes I seemed to be very close to that end. The doctors at Children's Hospital said they had to rewrite the medical books because of me. That's why my records take up a library of volumes instead of small folders. My doctors said they prayed for me. Later they even called me a miracle. My story is very powerful.

All my friends, family, school, church, town and everybody stood by me 110%. My Mom's favorite saying is, "If you want to see how good God is, look at my Candy Kisses."

My dream is that someday they will find a cure for cancer, so people won't have to go through what I had to endure. You don't appreciate what you have until suddenly you don't have it or it is taken from you. People just aren't thankful enough. I believe you should say a prayer of thanks every time you are able to drink a sip of water, walk or even when you are able to lie down in the bathtub to soak. Those things and many other things were taken from me for a long time. Things we take for granted are all gifts and blessings from God and can be taken away from us in a blink of the eye.

Because of my story I hope you will also find faith and hope and know that because I survived you can also. If you feel like you are drowning and need a lifeguard, try mine; he walks on water.

God is good! He allowed me to live for a special reason and I'll be ready to do whatever he has planned for me. *"So, look out world, here I come!!"*

—*Candy*

**Mary Ellen Sparks,
otherwise known as Mom**

A word from Mom

Candy's illness seemed never ending and it hurt so badly. Our whole life was changed in a moment and each day was worse than the day before. Pain and helplessness were so heavy on our shoulders. Everything went wrong with Candy. She went rock bottom but we went rock bottom right along with her.

In my Bible under the chapter of Luke 8:41-42, 48-56 I have written in red: *"Candy's story."* Candy is truly *"My Miracle from God"* as well as my hero. My little girl touched more lives than you can imagine. Come with us on this journey and discover the faith that kept my young daughter alive. See and feel what it is like to have a miracle happen. It worked for us and it's my prayer that it will work for whatever chapter in your life you are going through right now. We pray that God will bless you as you read this book.

—Mom

Recommendation from Judith Biddle

Sometimes in our walk through this life we reach a mountain so tall that we can't climb over it. We can't bypass the mountain because it blocks our path even though we must travel on.

Candy Kisses, My Miracle from God is about such a mountain and how one mother climbed over to the other side.

I can't imagine hearing the words, "She's gone." Mary's mountain was the illness of her only daughter who was eleven years old at the time she was stricken with leukemia. During the next three years Mary, her husband Bobby and son Jason spent more time at the hospital than they spent at home. But Mary found how to cross that mountain and tell their heartbreaking story. None of the journey was easy. The fact is, sometimes Mary was crawling rather than walking but she found her way across.

This book is a must-read for anyone who has come face to face with an insurmountable mountain, no matter what that mountain may be. Mary found the way to cross that mountain and find a modern miracle. In this book she shares with you how it can be done.

I highly recommend Candy Kisses to all who need a miracle.

Mary's sister,
Judith Biddle
Author: Tennessee Valley Echoes

Prologue

My precious grandson, Cody Dallas, sits next to me and says, "Mims, let's read together." His one-year-old little baby sister, Ally, follows suit and climbs up in my lap beside him. The book falls open as I read aloud from Susan Elizabeth Beck's *God Loves Me Baby Bible Board Book.* As I read to them, little Ally kisses the pictures in the book. Hot tears stream down my face as I read these words to them.

> **A little girl was very sick--in fact,
> she even died.
> Then Jesus came and took her hand,
> and made her come alive.
> God loved the little girl.**

I had to read the verse over again. Memories came flooding back.Those words described perfectly the life of my daughter, Candy. Candy Kisses, that's what we have called her since birth. Now I call her **"Candy Kisses, My Miracle from God."**

Our Journey

JOHN 11:25

April through July

Candy Kisses, My Miracle From GOD--the beginning

There go those four words again. The words seem to be rolling around in the air.

Your daughter has leukemia. I turn to my right to face my big good-looking husband, Bobby, and that dreadful look of hurt in his sky blue eyes. This has to be a dream. I'm trying to wake myself up, to come away from this awful nightmare...

"Mrs. Sparks, Mrs. Sparks, Are you OK? Do you understand what I have just told you?"

Tuesday, April Fool's Day, I had left work early to take Candy for a follow-up visit to her pediatrician, Dr. Bearman. Two weeks earlier Candy had found three small knots in the gland of her throat. She had finished fourteen days of antibodies, didn't act sick nor had she slowed down at all. Saturday we had gone fishing all day to celebrate her Dad's birthday and Sunday she played and danced as she helped do yard work. Then, on Sunday night we noticed the bruises. What was it her Daddy had said quietly to me the night before? "You would have to throw Candy against a brick wall to make those types of bruises. I'm afraid of leukemia."

Because of the bruises, Candy was afraid our pediatrician, Dr. Bearman, would accuse us of child abuse. But Dr. Bearman knew Candy was our precious little girl whom we had always been so protective of. Hey, we're the ones who watch out through the window each time Candy walks next door to see her Aunt Lucy. We have always been afraid someone would grab her and take her away from us or that she would be hurt in some way. Yes, we are overly protective but Candy is so special, petite, pretty and how she brightens our lives with her dancing, singing and cheerful attitude. Sitting in the exam room waiting to see our pediatrician, Dr. Bearman, I recalled how Candy had broken her elbow less than a year before during 6ᵗʰ grade cheerleading practice. She was barely eleven then and it had been so hard getting her through that terrible ordeal. Candy always had been the type that got nervous and cried at just the mention of a shot.

After a blood test, Dr. Bearman made the arrangements for a Dr. Berkow to meet us at Children's Hospital. He wouldn't even let us go home to pack. As we left his office, Dr. Bearman hugged us. I noticed a tear fall from his eyes. With shaky hands, I called my husband from the car. At Children's Hospital, Dr. Berkow, with his Looney Tunes tie and Nurse Meredith greeted us. Both friendly faces were very familiar.

I said, "Hey Dr. Berkow, you know Candy's daddy, Bobby. He's on the Camp Smile-A-Mile board of directors with you and we all know and love Nurse Meredith from camp."

I felt comfort in knowing Candy was in good hands. Candy, who was so scared of needles, had just had an IV started in her little arm, her big eyes still teary. It felt like forever until her Daddy and big bubba Jason arrive at the hospital. My sister, Evelyn, and my best friend, Cat, made it to the hospital before we did so they agreed to stay close to Candy as the doctors ushered us three, Mom, Dad and Brother into a conference room at the end of the hall.

There go those four words again floating around in the air: Your daughter has leukemia.

No, don't they know. This can't be happening to us. We have always been on the other side of the fence. For eight years, we have been avid supporters of Camp Smile-A-Mile, a special camp for children with cancer. My best friend Cathy and I made over $28,000 in only a few months selling red clown noses for the camp. Everyone wore their clown noses on April Fool's Day. Cathy and I had traveled all over the state promoting the camp video and pulling in supporters. Jeff Cook of the Alabama Band hosted a commercial on television with us wearing our red noses. The next year Cathy and I raised over $18,000 on the red noses for the Camp Smile-A Mile. How ironic.

We even have pictures of us going to Montgomery to have Governor Guy Hunt sign a proclamation stating April 1st as official Red Nose Day for Camp Smile-A-Mile, a camp for children with cancer. I'm part of the Telephone Pioneers. We rent buses and carry all the campers to McDonald's for happy meals before each camp. We even purchased the camp a new van with the Camp Smile-A Mile red monkey logo on it. We paid for a new boy's dorm. We take our clowns, have carnivals, dances, parties, etc. for the children with cancer. Candy and Jason have been clowns at the camp. Hey, don't they realize I was President of the Telephone Pioneers? My council raised over $200,000 in on year to help hundreds of different organizations in need. No, there has to be some mistake. Me, Bobby, Jason and Candy, we help other people in need. It can't happen to us. Bobby is on the board of directors for Camp Smile-A-Mile. He works at Alltel and they purchased the camp a golf cart for the children. Don't they know? This can't be happening to us!

How Ironic! Today is April 1st—Red Nose Day for Camp Smile-A-Mile . . .

April Fool's Day . . . How Ironic! .

They can't try to tell us our child has leukemia. There has to be some mistake.

Thus begins three long years . . .

Meet Ora Mae, our God-sent nurse

God places certain people in your life to help you on your journey through devastating chapters of your life. As our journey began on April 1st, you can only imagine what a relief and comfort we felt that first day moving Candy from the emergency room into a room on the fifth floor of Children's Hospital and

Candy as 6th grade cheerleader

immediately having Ora Mae appear in our lives. Candy's dad knew Ora Mae, her husband Larry and her whole family very well. Ora Mae put her arms around us in a group hug, holding onto Bobby the longest.

Ora Mae began asking us all the required questions on that long form on her clipboard. Candy being a little ball of fire answered the questions for us.

Candy giggled when Ora Mae asked, "Do you have indoor plumbing?"

Candy's giggling wasn't what got Ora Mae's attention. It was the answer Candy replied to when asked, "What is your religious preference?"

Candy didn't even have to think or pause as she quickly answered, "**Jesus.**" We noticed Ora Mae turn her clipboard upside down and look upward at the ceiling for a few silent seconds, as if she were in deep thought.

Ora Mae's eyes looked glassy as she blinked back a tear and said, "I have waited my whole life to hear someone give the answer of **Jesus.**"

Ora Mae went home from work that night crying and told her family that her greatest fear had come true. She later told us that her greatest fear in being a nurse was that one day a child of a close friend from her own hometown would appear on her fifth floor Hematology/Oncology Unit with cancer and she would have to treat that child. On that day, we were Ora Mae's greatest fear.

Let Bubba go in with me

Next day, standing outside the small surgery room with tears burning my eyes, memories came flooding back as **I had a flashback of how big brother Jason had always been there for Candy.** In my mind, I suddenly saw Candy again with a broken elbow less than a year earlier during cheerleading practice. I remembered another parent running toward me and saying that Candy was hurt bad. I remember running down the hillside to where the young cheerleaders were gathered in a circle around my Candy. Her elbow was twisted in such a fashion that it looked like it wasn't even attached. My heart seemed to drop out of my chest. I remember Candy's eyes were big with fear and with her dirty hand she wiped the tears from her face as she repeated over and over, "I want my Bubba. I want my Bubba."

All her young life, she had always wanted her big brother whenever she hurt herself or was afraid. Jason was the one Candy always wanted. That day last year looking down at Candy with her broken elbow, a shudder of fear overtook me and I remember I ran to my car to get my phone. I must have looked stricken, disoriented and down right confused as to what to do. Out of nowhere, Candy's brother, Jason, appeared in the cab of his candy apple red newly restored 1964 Chevy truck.

Hanging out the window, I remember him shouting out to me, "What's wrong, Mom? What has happened?"

I looked at him puzzled, because it was so strange that Jason had suddenly appeared just when Candy had needed him. He had no way of knowing that Candy had been hurt. Jason had been with his Dad working over at our farm when for some unknown reason he had an incredible unexplainable urge to drive up to the school. He said, "Dad, I'll be back. I gotta go." That was unusual for Jason. He always stayed around to help finish up. There was no reason for him to go to the school that day, but for some unknown reason he headed straight there as if he had been beckoned. Jason is six and half years older than Candy but they seem to have a special bond. Broken elbow, eleven years old, she needed and was crying for her Bubba and all at once he was there for her. I remembered watching Jason scoop little Candy up in his strong arms. As tears streamed down her dirty face she put her good arm around his neck and kissed his cheek. He carried her to my car and we raced to the emergency room. It was so hard getting Candy through that terrible ordeal of a broken elbow less than a year before.

As my mind comes away from that awful flashback I wonder how we will ever manage leukemia. Here we are outside the surgery room. Candy always had been the type that even the mention of a needle made her nervous and cry and here we were fixing to have a very painful seven-part bone marrow spinal test to determine what kind of leukemia Candy was facing. Candy didn't want Mom and Daddy going in with her. She would be awake during the procedure. As always, she cuddled close to Jason and said, "Let Bubba go in with me to hold me." So there we stood, our shoulders drooping, our hearts breaking as big brother, Jason, carried his little sister, Candy, inside for the first of many painful procedures. This was a seven- part spinal tap where the fluid would be tested to tell us what kind of leukemia we were facing. How brave our little girl was. How helpless and afraid her mom and dad felt standing outside the door.

Daddy, please don't cry!!

Again the very next day after that first seven-part bone marrow spinal test we found ourselves again going through a second very painful spinal tap. This time the fluid drawn out would be replaced with chemo shot into Candy's spine to begin her treatments to save her life. How this tugs at your heart. We feel so afraid and helpless for our little girl. Mom and Dad would be brave this time and we wanted to go in with our little girl to help her through this terrible ordeal.

Big brother, Jason, waited heavy-hearted outside the door this time. He asked, "Mom, are you sure you wouldn't prefer for me to go in with her?"

Daddy held his little girl close to his chest for the procedure. I stood behind him.

Our special nurse had trouble getting the fluid out of Candy's spine. It was an awfully big needle and they had to try several different ways before they were successful. Candy saw me cry a lot but I'll never forget her saying, "**Daddy, please don't cry**!" Daddy wiped away a burning tear from his tear-filled eyes.

For all the many future very painful spinal taps that Candy had, Mom and Daddy decided it wasn't so good for us to try to be brave. Instead, we let Jason go in with Candy. She was always awake for each procedure and Bubba always made it better when he held her.

Our lives put on hold as we literally live in the hospital

This morning I tried to hide my silent tears but as I stood over the sink my tears fell softly into my dishwater. I realized it had been less than three weeks since Candy was diagnosed and we had already spent ten days in the hospital. Being readmitted soon became the norm. Today was April 19th and we had to rush Candy back to the hospital. This time we would be there until June 4th. We moved in with her, staying by her side the whole time. We decided we would put our lives on hold and do whatever it took to keep our precious little daughter alive. The helplessness and the overwhelming sense of grief were almost more than we could stand. The hospital put us in a bigger room than normal. I guess they realized that Mom, Dad and Jason would be stuck to Candy like glue. We bought twin bed rubber foam pads to place in the chairs in Candy's room for us to sleep on. Each chair folded out to make a sleeping recliner.

Every day was worse than the day before. Sometimes we would go all day long and remember late that night that we hadn't even taken time to eat. Precious caring friends brought us books and magazines to read; however, our minds wouldn't allow us to focus long enough to read anything. Our pastor, Brother LeCroy, came to visit us every couple of days. He always seemed to walk through the door just the time we needed him most. He often held Bobby in a hug because it was especially hard on a daddy when there is nothing he can do to make things right.

Our God-sent nurse, Ora Mae, was never far away. Talk about having the right connections. Wow! Ora Mae had the connections. She could get things moving when no one else could. How many times we watched as Ora Mae put her connections to work in fast gear. By connections, I mean Ora Mae had a direct line to God up above. Each time we needed something and needed it really fast to keep Candy alive, Ora Mae got the prayer line going in fast motion. We have been totally amazed at how God would send the exact thing we needed, just in the exact time needed because the prayer line got activated. Some of the prayers came immediately, some were answered in ways that we hadn't anticipated and some answers would seem to drag out and come across at the last moment. The answers were never too late. I have never seen anything so powerful.

One day a lady and her husband came to visit us and pray for Candy. Bobby knew the lady because she worked at a big local car auction and he had met her while working on their phone system. I will never forget what she said to me, "**If God isn't moving, get prayers going and move God.**"

That sounded so strange to me. I wondered, **"Can you really move God?"**

Ora Mae knew you could move God and she and her prayer chain got God moving time and time again. She had a direct line into God's ear. She never received a busy signal; she used that direct line in faith, expecting results. Ora Mae has strong shoulders which are really good to cry upon. She especially held up Bobby. A daddy is suppose to be able to fix everything that goes wrong with his children and this daddy soon realized that he couldn't fix it. It is devastating for a daddy not to be able to make things better for his little girl. It hurts beyond measure.

Candy developed disseminated candidiasis

Every day was worse than the day before. You think nothing else can go wrong but the next day doctors give an announcement of something else totally unforeseen that has bottomed out.

After about a week in the hospital, we noticed Candy was breaking out with red bumps.

After a blood test was taken, during the middle of the night, we were scared to death when the nurses came rushing in and started an emergency IV medication for a yeast and bacteria infection.

Early the next morning they took Candy to the small surgery room and she was awake while they did two things. Of course, her big Bubba Jason went right in with her to hold her close to him. Mom and Dad had gotten use to standing outside this same door with hot tears burning their cheeks. Biopsy one was to remove a small piece of skin from above Candy's inside thigh just above her knee area. In years to come she would refer to this scar as her little bug. Second biopsy was preformed through her back to test a small piece of her lung. We waited for the results.

The next day I had gone home to take a bath and change clothes and Bobby called from the hospital to tell me they were rushing Candy into the ICU. Jason and I rushed back to the hospital. I remember crying so hard because I thought Candy was dying. That old devil not only got us down but now he was stomping all over us. It hurt more than you could ever imagine. We couldn't do anything but accept all the bad news.

There was only one room that parents could rent and it was at the end of the hall where the ICU was. It had only a couch that made into a bed, a TV and bathtub. No toilet in the room; we had to go down the hall to the public restroom. You could only reserve the room for three nights at a time then you had to relinquish it if another parent needed to rent it. If necessary, we would have slept on the floor outside the ICU doors; however, we were very grateful when we did have the room. At that time, we didn't know how much the room rented for or even if it would be available. We hoped they would take a check because going to the bank had not even entered our minds. Something incredible happened. A church in our community came by and Pastor Johnny Stewart folded an envelope in the palm of my hand. I thanked him through teary eyes. Pastor Johnny put his hand over my hand as he prayed the sweetest prayer not only for Candy's healing but for strength and comfort for Mom, Dad and Brother. He said he didn't know how much money was in the envelope; only that his congregation had taken up a love offering that night for us.

It wasn't until later than night that Kay Free, our social worker, came by and told us that we had the room reserved for three nights and told us how much it cost. Suddenly, I remembered the envelope that Pastor Johnny had put in my hand. When I opened the envelope, it was like someone had just given me a warm hug because as I counted out loud the money in the envelope and handed it to Kay I found it contained the exact amount we needed plus fifty cents over. Bobby and I looked at each other in amazement at the envelope that had exactly the right amount to reserve the room and enough left over for a candy bar. Wow, what a special candy kiss from God.

One of us would sleep for a couple of hours or I should say, try to sleep, then relieve the other one that had stayed by Candy's bedside in the ICU. Her little body was so fragile that the doctors got Candy an air bed to sleep on. The next day, as the nurses changed shifts, Bobby and I needed a quick break so we walked down to the cafeteria together. When we came back, I went into an emotional turmoil when I could see through the small curtain opening in Candy's ICU room that the doctors were putting an emergency IV into Candy's groin area. They said it was necessary to save Candy's life. Candy was awake and we could see the fear in her eyes. Candy's look of terror seemed to fade when she saw her daddy through the opening in the curtain. She raised her little hand from under the cover and gave us half a wave. They wouldn't allow us to go in until the procedure was finished so we cried outside the curtains. We chewed them out for doing that while we slipped away for just a few minutes and told them not to touch her again without one of us being there. We felt like we should have been allowed to hold her hand while they put that IV in her groin area. Being the professionals they were, they never got ugly or mean with us and we knew in our hearts that they thought they would have the procedure finished by the time we came back in. They had tried to spare us some pain. For us to come back early and be able to see the look of fear in Candy's eyes through the small opening in the curtains was unbearable.

Test results showed Candy had disseminated candidiasis, which is a slow growing fungus or yeast infection in her bloodstream. It wasn't long before the heart lesion was found. A leaky mitral value, referred to as a hole in her heart, was pumping all this very serious fungal infection from her heart to all her vital organs, including her liver, kidneys, spleen, brain and also behind her eyes. This dangerous infection was more deadly than the leukemia.

So, as the leukemia took second place to this deadly infection, the doctors from the UAB Department of Forensic Science, sometimes referred to as the Infectious Disease Center, took over Candy's treatment. Her treatments for leukemia were put on hold, on the back burner. She now had to endure a four-hour treatment each day intravenously for this deadly infection. She was given the strongest most aggressive medicines available to save her life. She had to be pre-medicated with high doses of Tylenol and Benadryl before each treatment. Most people who get this deadly infection live less than a week. We were told that Candy may not make it through the night. Candy would end up battling this serious disease for nine months. A feeding tube was put down her throat the next day.

One of us was always by Candy's ICU bedside day and night. I remember one of the night nurses telling me that she would allow one person to sit next to Candy's bed during the night time hours but we had better not go to sleep and we had to leave temporarily in the morning during nurses' shift change. If we went to sleep we had to leave the room because she didn't need two patients to take care of. Candy had one dedicated nurse who never left her sight all night.

She totally belonged to Candy and her purpose was to keep Candy alive. We thankfully agreed with her instructions and we noticed that she gave our little girl much gentle loving care all night long. Her focus never left Candy. I was the one who usually stayed during night hours with Bobby swapping places with me after the early morning nurse shift change. Being so tired and exhausted made it really hard to stay awake. Sometimes I would nod off to sleep, maybe even snore then almost fall off the tall stool. I would quickly grab hold of the railing and try to appear wide awake. I would steal a look at our nurse, who always pretended not to see me. Often my best friend, Cat, would stay the night by Candy's bedside so we could catch a few hours sleep in the rented room down the hall. When nurses' shift change came and we relieved Cat of her duties, she would go from the hospital straight to work. Everyone should have a Cat in their lives, a God-given Cat.

Sometimes the Lord calms the storm; sometimes He lets the storm rage and calms His Child.

Fear Not

Candy was moved temporarily back into a regular room. Candy ran a fever of 103 on Mother's Day and the next two days she passed some blood in her stool. They did X-rays and scans and found nothing. They stopped her food tube and she was given more blood to build her up for surgery for the next day to put her central line in under her arm. Candy's veins had been all used up from IVs and this central line would keep her from having more IVs put in. Her medicines and treatments would be plugged into the central line rather than through an IV each time. The night before the surgery we were so afraid. They didn't know why

Candy was bleeding internally and they had prepared us to expect the worst while hoping for better.

It felt as if we were sitting on the edge of a cliff, leaning back in a chair that could be pulled from underneath us at any moment. So helpless we were. Late that night I went down to the break area and saw a Bible by a table. When I picked it up, it seemed the pages kept falling open to the words **Fear Not.** I didn't realize it at the time but there are **365 Fear Not** commands listed in the Bible. Everywhere I looked the words **Fear Not** seemed to be highlighted and jumping off the pages demanding my attention. I felt tranquil. When I went back up to the room I got next to Candy's bed and held her hand and with confidence I said, "Candy Kisses, you are going to be OK, I promise. God has just told me several times to fear not. I don't understand all this but I know that we must **Fear Not,** just hold on and see how this unfolds."

All four of us, Candy, Mom, Dad and Jason all agreed we would not be afraid. We would just hang in there. The next day when they came to get Candy for surgery I reminded her that we had agreed to **Fear Not.** She kissed us all then said, "I'm not afraid, Mom, see you in a few." Our little girl was so brave. She always kept a positive outlook. Her dimple always shining and all she wanted was to comfort us and keep us from hurting or worrying. As she left for surgery our hearts ached and our arms felt empty. We felt so helpless but we held on to our promise of **Fear Not**.

My preacher, Brother LeCroy, came through our door just in time to pray a quick prayer for Candy and to sit and wait with Mom and Dad. Dr. Cain, our surgeon called us on the room phone about five hours later to say the surgery when fine. The leakage in her heart and the bleeding internally was not as bad as they thought. The internal bleeding was caused from a cut made when they had pushed her feeding tube down her throat. One of her lungs had collapsed so she had to start breathing treatments to restore it. The next day they removed Candy's feeding tube from down her throat. Our eyes and our hearts were beginning to know that God was moving in to help us. Chains that seem to be binding us were slowly falling away. That felt so good.

Picture this

I often imagine myself sitting beside Jesus on a bench at Mt. Olive. I feel enveloped in a love so consuming that I almost get lost in it. I go there often when I need a warm hug to get me through a difficult time. Jesus is a good listener. I often lay my head upon his shoulder. Sometimes we just sit there in quiet peace and other times I have to pour my heart out to him. There have been times when I actually ran to him with the thought going through my head, **"I must tell Jesus, I cannot bear this burden alone."** Arms outstretched, he hugs my cares away.

Now picture this. The seat on the bench next to Jesus is empty. He's still there, quietly waiting for you. You can feel the warmth and sense the wonder of it all. As you look overhead the sky is crystal clear and you hear the birds singing praises of welcome. Colorful flowers outline the pathway leading to Jesus. The stones on the walkway are soft under your feet. You hear a stream of running water close by. The stillness of it all just seems to overflow and you feel so loved. It's as if Jesus has put the universe on hold. Rest assured he is still in perfect control. He, however, makes you feel like the most important person in the whole wide world. As you muster up the courage to sit next to him you feel so special, so loved. Your whole body, from the top of your head to the tip of your toes, feels so refreshed and energized. Sit down as the warm air envelopes you like a hug. Lay your head upon Jesus' shoulder. Rejoice and know that you can tell Jesus anything. Pour out your heart to him.

Jesus Christ the same yesterday, and today, and for ever.

—Hebrews 13:8 KJV

Candy's esophagus closes up

Just as we are beginning to get our heads above water we are hit with more bad news. How can things get any worse? What else can happen? I needed Mom and Dad (Candy's grandparents) but they were up in heaven. Once my sister, Evelyn, said, "Mary, our Mom and Dad couldn't have handled this situation and besides they have more power now than before. They can approach the throne directly in your behalf." Also my pastor, whom we love so much, Brother Norman, was always near. His wife once told me that he would come back from the hospital and cry as he prayed for Candy. It just seemed to go on forever, never ending. I remember our cousin, Michael, who was a newly ordained minister saying, "I have prayed and I have prayed. I don't understand what is taking God so long. He is going to heal Candy, which I have no doubts about. I'm holding God to that healing. I just don't know why God is dragging this out so long." I pulled lots of strength from Michael and from him I was taught that you can hold God to what he has promised you, even though you cannot see it unfolding. You must never doubt that it will happen in God's perfect timing.

In addition to the four-hour intravenous treatment needed every day to fight this deadly infection, Candy also had to take two huge what we referred to as "horse capsules" twice a day by mouth. Now we were faced with a new dilemma as Candy's little body began rejecting the large capsules. First the doctors had the capsules mixed with ice cream so Candy could swallow them. Then Candy got where she could no longer get the capsules down and she hated the taste of that ice cream. Next they decided to mix the capsules with cherry syrup hoping to force them down her throat. Soon that no longer worked. Bobby said, "Mary, it's like God is trying to tell us that Candy's body does not need those capsules."

Then God made the unthinkable happened. Candy's esophagus closed up. He really got our attention then. She would now require being put to sleep every couple of weeks for esophagus dilatation. This would continue for many months, even after we were able to go home. The doctors warned us that Candy may never be able to eat again by mouth, that her esophagus might not ever open up enough to eat by mouth. They sent her to surgery to get a Mic-Key skin level feeding tube installed in her stomach through her abdominal wall. There was an inflatable balloon at one end and an external base at the other. This tube would allow intake of foods and water and a means to take her medicine through this stomach feeding tube.

Their new plan was that the capsules would now be mixed with water and put into a tube that fed directly into her stomach. Her esophagus would not be involved. We also began feeding Candy cans of liquid food through her feeding tube in her stomach. Then the unthinkable happened again. This time Candy's Mic-Key feeding tube in her stomach clogged up. Nothing could be forced down that tube into her stomach. It just wouldn't work. They replaced the feeding tube but each time it would clog up again. Then the inflatable balloon that was used to keep the tube in place suddenly began to deflate as her body pushed the Mic-Key feeding tube out. They tried to

inflate the balloon again. They replaced it with another new Mic-Key tube. Still her body kept pushing the device out of her stomach. Her body just would not tolerate that feeding tube being in her stomach. With a sigh Bobby said, "Mary, God is trying to tell us something and we just aren't listening. First we mixed the capsules with ice cream, then cherry syrup, then when we still did not listen God closes her esophagus up. What else does God have to do to get our attention? Candy's body does not need those capsules. So instead of listening after her esophagus closes up what do we do but force those capsules down a tube in her belly. Well, now God has clogged that feeding tube up. The balloon won't stay inflated. Now her body keeps pushing the feeding tube out. It won't stay in any longer. She doesn't need those capsules. I think those capsules are killing her. Why can't we get the doctors to take her off them? How else can God stop us from giving her those capsules?" Angrily, I picked up those last two capsules and threw them in the toilet. A few hours later those capsules had literally exploded and they were five times bigger, now the size of apples. Bobby and I were amazed. We made up our minds that somehow we would take her off those capsules. Our doctors and nurses felt they couldn't change things because the Infectious Disease Center was in charge. They made the ground rules and no one could override their decisions. Then one of our senior doctors from our Oncology Department came through our door and pulled up a chair to sit and talk with us. We showed him the exploded capsules in the toilet. Can you imagine how they had also been exploding in her little stomach? He listened to what Bobby had to say and he said,
     "**I can change things**. I don't have to have anyone's approval. Actually I don't see any proof that those capsules are working. So as of now Candy is officially

off them." Thank you, God, for doctors who listen. Now off those capsules, Candy began to improve immensely. Her liquid food now went down her Mic-Key feeding tube. It was no longer clogged up. God knew Candy's body did not need those capsules. Those capsules were killing her. God went to great lengths to make us take action. What a patient loving heavenly father we have. He tried one way to get our attention, then another way and he kept on until we finally listened to him. He was in control the whole time, not the doctors.

Candy, Mom, and Oink

Surgery was required every couple of weeks for esophageal dilatation. Candy was put to sleep each time. Candy had a TY pink pig Beanie Baby pillow pal which she had nicknamed Oink. All the nurses knew Oink and allowed her to hold him during each dilatation. They always let Candy choose which flavor scent she wanted for the air she would breathe that would put her into a deep sleep before the surgery plus they also gave her lip balm of the same flavor. She was always joking and laughing with the nurses as they wheeled her bed into the surgery room. She usually chose root beer or chocolate scent. It never got easy for us, waiting for her to return. Tears always filled Mom, Dad and Jason's eyes each time as we watched her disappear through the surgery doors. Oink and Jesus always went with her to keep her company.

Faith is trusting in something that will only make sense in reverse.

Ora Mae goes to school to talk leukemia to the students

Meanwhile life goes on; or at least it goes on for everyone else. It seemed to have stopped for us. The students and teachers from Candy's school wanted to stay very much involved in Candy's life. We couldn't have made it without our nurse and close friend, Ora Mae. While we were literally living in the hospital, Ora Mae went to Candy's school and held a big conference in the gym explaining to the student body exactly what Candy was battling. She answered all their questions and addressed their fears including, "Do children Candy's age die from leukemia?" Because she did that, the entire school got behind her 110%. Students sent us boxes of homemade cards, balloons, stuffed animals and little keepsake love items.

Students would gather in the halls to pray for Candy. Support overflowing and love outpouring was shown for us by the teachers and students. Her 6th grade class collected money to buy her a fish aquarium when she returned home. They thought it would help her and give her peace to watch fish. We kept all those priceless treasures and still have them stored in five big plastic containers. Here's some of the items we got: sandcastle, dream catcher, turtle, frog, Macarena dancing teddy bear, big leopard cub stuffed animal, small love is for sharing bear, angel figurine, little bear in a bag, wind chimes, angle pin, Mickey Mouse vase with flowers, sun catcher window decoration, clown, journal, two pairs of shorts, seal pup, fatso big pup, laughing happy face, Brita water filter, Mickey Mouse hat, lamb with cross, mustard seed pens, guardian angel wind chime, snowman, big basket with eleven beanie babies, unicorn bean collection, hug me talking bear, bear key chain imprinted with Candy on it, Dalmatian pup, beanie mouse, snoopy big soft dog, porcelain ballerina doll, JB Bean collector bear with glasses, T-shirt with kids' colorful painted handprints, big fruit baskets, apple mini tea set, heart bracelet, family reunion animal puzzle, lamp with cross, bean bag rag, wishbone dog and seal, unicorn bean bag, happy birthday bear in a bag, barking dog, purse heart mirror, ceramic cross, Chia pet, pink and blue monkey, books, homemade clown, homemade quilt, computer games, Precious Moments hug-a-bear, musical angel box, shells from Florida, Tennessee Aquarium T-shirt, Lee Ann Rimes sound track, etc. We kept all those priceless treasures from Candy's loving classmates and we still have them stored in five big plastic containers. Since it was the Beanie Babies era, one huge plastic container is full of TY collectible Beanie Babies. We treasure all those gifts given to Candy out of love, especially those handmade cards. One day we hope Candy will be able to sit down maybe with her own little girl and hold all those items in her hands and still feel the love that was sent her way by all her fellow students. That thought brings tears to our eyes and warms our hearts.

Give, and it will be given to you. A good measure, pressed down, shaken together and running over will be poured into your lap.

—Luke 6:38 NIV

Union made prayers go straight up to God

I stand amazed and humble at all the people God sent to help us. When Candy was born our union news letter announced her birth as UNION MADE because Dad and Mom both were long time union members. That term union made came around full circle as unions from all over the United States came to our rescue. Ton loads of prayers, cards and telephone calls came in through our local under the watch and direction of our president and secretary/treasurer. Our local even sent the thank you letters on our behalf. This was long before Facebook or Twitter.

In addition to telecommunication workers, there were government employees, building, construction, maintenance, glass, molders, pottery, plastic workers, theatrical, electrical workers, longshoremen's, teachers, plumbers, steamfitters, state employees, pipe fitters, carpenters, food, commercial, paper workers, steelworkers and more. Our union sent us copies of those thank you letters that they sent out for us and we literally have stacks of them from all around the United States. We cherish them all. We thank God for these caring unions. **Can you imagine all the union made prayers that had been going up to heaven for our little girl?** The way God's people come forth to give in time of need with their love and prayers is totally amazing. We serve an awesome God with endless resources, power and love. It brings me to my knees with thankfulness.

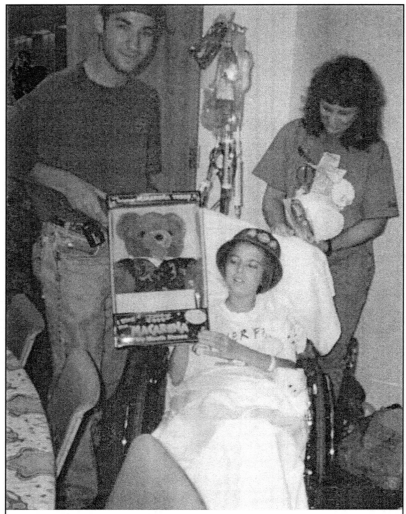

12th birthday party in hospital with Mom & Jason

If I could sit on the porch with God, the first thing I would do is thank him for you!

Candy's 12th birthday and students give her a blood drive

Turning twelve years old is a special time for girls. They are growing up, becoming independent, making new friends, exploring new adventures and giggling all the time about their dreams and desires which have now begun to include the cute boys they meet every day. At their 12th birthday party they should dance, laugh, open presents and maybe even kiss a boy for the first time. Candy could do none of this. She was in the hospital battling every day for her life. She was too sick to ask, "Why me? Why can't I be doing all the exciting things other kids are able to do?"

The nurses on the 5th floor of Children's Hospital did give Candy two very special birthday parties. We had to put Candy in a wheelchair to take her to each party. That was one of the few times she wore a hat and I believe it was because she was too sick to object. The day shift nurses gave her a party and then the night shift nurses gave her another party. The conference room held colorful balloons, two beautiful decorated cakes and presents galore filled the room. Candy was so sick and weak. You could tell that everyone there doubted that she would ever see her 13th birthday. Still they sang and laughed and put on two great parties for Candy. She tried to appear happy and told them all how very much she loved them. Thank you, God, for each of those caring loving nurses who fell in love with our Candy and took such good care of her. They also took very good care of Mom, Dad and brother Jason. While we lived in the hospital they became our family.

On Candy's birthday, our pain was so raw and hurt so deep but somewhere deep down inside us something kept us fighting and pushing forward to a new day awakening when all this would be behind us. It just seemed never ending, like a nightmare that you were trying to wake up from or like a scary movie you were watching about someone else. Still, we tried to be brave for Candy. All the time she was the brave one with her cracking jokes and singing funny tunes. She always brought smiles to everyone's faces. She never complained or fussed. I often wondered how people in the outside world could be going on with their everyday life when ours was in such turmoil. Going through what our family had to endure makes you see life in a whole different perspective. Things that make people mad and angry seem so trivial when you have to battle every day to keep your young precious daughter alive.

Because Candy was in the hospital really sick on her 12th birthday, the students from her school held a very successful blood drive to show support for Candy. It was their way of thanking all the people who had donated the blood that had saved Candy's life. Over 100 people showed up to donate blood and sign two giant get-well soon cards. The Red Cross was so impressed that the next day they came to the hospital and presented Candy with a white bear with a red cross on it. They were amazed at how successful her fellow students were in sponsoring the blood drive. Thank God for the students and all the community who rolled up their sleeves to donate life-saving blood at the blood drive in Candy's honor.

A couple of years later, I called the Red Cross for information and this number will astonish you. To save Candy's life she was given 40 units of blood and 9 pints of platelets at various times. One pint of platelets equates to 10-12 randomly donated units of whole red blood. The Red Cross estimated 136-148 pints of blood donated by individuals was used to keep

Students show support with Birthday Blood Drive

By Kimberly Stark
THE LEEDS NEWS

Tomorrow (May 23) a little girl in Odenville will turn 12. For most little girls this would be just another birthday as they headed toward being a teenager, but for Candy Sparks this is a special birthday.

On April 1, 1997 Candy was diagnosed as having Acute Lymphothatic Leukemia. She will celebrate this birthday at Children's Hospital in Birmingham where she is undergoing chemotherapy to treat the leukemia. Even though she wont be home to have a party. All of her sixth grade classmates at St. Clair County High School will be celebrating for her in a very special way. They will hold a special Birthday Blood Drive for Candy. The drive will take place on Tuesday, May 27 from 2:00 p.m. until 6:00 p.m.

According to Candy's mother, Mary Sparks, the students decided to hold the drive in order to not only show Candy that they support her but in order to help others. "After meeting with one of Candy's nurses, Ora Mae Layton, the kids learned how much leukemia patients need platelets and other blood products," said Sparks. "The kids wanted to do it (blood drive) to save other people's lives, like those who gave the blood that has been used to save Candy's life."

"The kids were real receptive," said Layton, when asked how Candy's classmates responded to her coming to talk to them about Candy. "They asked questions that most people only wonder and are afraid to ask, especially people their age," She said they all wanted to know the details of Candy's disease. She told them that Leukemia is a disease that attacks the White Blood Cells and makes them grow uncontrollably. The children also wanted to know if children their age died. "Kids that age think they are indispensable. You just have to tell them the truth, that yes sometimes children that age die," Layton feels that if you lie to a child the first time then when something bad does happen then they wont believe you again. She keeps in touch with the teachers at the school and they in turn let the students know what is happening with Candy. "The kids have been really been wonderful," said Layton. "They have really rallied for her."

Sparks states that the students at the school have been so supportive of their classmate. "We were told that the students asked for a chance to gather and pray for Candy," said Sparks. "Sometimes a group of them will even get together in the hall and pray for her." She said she has sent word through a prayer line at one of the churches what her daughter needs, such as platelets. "It seems like as soon as people start praying, Candy gets what she needs," said Sparks. "The support we have had in Odenville has been amazing. I've never seen a town spiritually pull together like this one has."

Sparks said that while this has been a tough situation to go through, the wonderful prayers and thoughts from the community have worked miracles to help them get through this. "We've been by Candy's side night and day since we came to the hospital,"said Sparks. "Not only have the students supported us, but the principal also came by the hospital and presented Candy with an award she was suppose to receive for being in the top five in her class." Candy is a straight A student. According to her mother she has never made a B on her report card.

Candy is what most people would consider an all around active student and preteen. She is a cheerleader for the sixth grade. "She is for ever wanting to learn new things," said Sparks. "So much so that we bought her a computer for Christmas. She loves to make flyers and stuff on it." She also loves to swim, fish and do lots of outdoor activities. "The day before we went into the hospital,"said Sparks, "she was out in the font yard cleaning up."

Candy and her family have been active with Camp Smile-a-mile for the last eight years. Her dad, Bobby Sparks, is on the camp's board of directors. "We were always on the other side (of cancer),"said Sparks. "Then all at once we found ourselves on this side. We soon found out how devastating and how much this hurts, which is more than you can imagine."

Candy was diagnosed with Leukemia after finding three lumps in her glands in her throat. However, she never slowed down or acted sick until after she was diagnosed stated her mom. "She's been in good spirits the whole time," said Sparks. "But lately she's been real tired and worn out. But she always seems to keep her sense of humor."

It is unknown how much longer Candy will be in the hospital. She will be undergoing chemotherapy for at least the next six months stated her mom. "Right now they say she's in remission," said Sparks. "They will have to watch her for the next two years to make sure it's gone."

—Birthday Blood Drive Leeds News—
To celebrate Candy's birthday the community rallied together and over 200 people donated blood for Candy.

Candy alive. Thank God for those 136-148 people who gave the gift of blood that saved our daughter.

Bright red candy kisses

Candy was always thanking the doctors, nurses and everyone that she came in contact with. The words "I love you" were always flowing from her heart to her lips. She even told the housekeeping staff who picked up the trash and the ones who delivered her dinner trays that she loved them. She won everyone over. She had a roll of red lip stickers that looked like giant kisses. Everyone she came in contact with was given a red lipstick kiss sticker to wear either on their name tag or clothes. It seems those stickers were everywhere throughout the hospital. They symbolized her love, her very own brand of candy kisses. Nurses, doctors, chaplains, housekeeping workers, lunch room workers, X-ray techs, lab workers, etc. all wore her kiss stickers.

Most people were amazed that even Dr. Cain who had put Candy's central line in wore a candy kiss. Dr. Cain was a senior doctor, very much respected and somewhat feared by all. Everyone said he was the best surgeon there. He was tough and no one ever crossed him. His word was the law and people seemed to tiptoe around him. I think he kind of liked that reputation.

We loved Dr. Cain. Thank God for his expertise. We were very grateful when he put Candy's central line in under her arm. No one could believe it but somehow little Candy wiggled herself right into Dr. Cain's heart as he proudly displayed his very own kiss sticker every day on his name tag. People were amazed.

Surprisingly, there was only one person who for some unknown reason didn't get one of Candy's kiss stickers. She just didn't like that nurse who was borrowed from another floor. We got really tickled at

Candy one evening when that nurse left our room. Candy, who never said a negative word against

Mailbox

Dear Editor

On April 1, 1997 our daughter, Candy, was diagnosed with Acute Lymphotholic Leukemia. While struggling with this terrible disease she also developed a very serious fungal infection in her blood stream. The infection called Candida spread from her heart to all her vital organs including her liver, kidneys, spleen, brain and behind her eyes. Candy has been in Children's Hospital almost continuously from April 1 until July 4, 1997.

We (her Mom and Dad) have both been on leave of absence from work the whole time to stay night and day by her side. Candy continues to receive chemo for the leukemia, which is in remission. She also receives an intravenous four hour treatment each day for the fungus infection. Candy now has a temporary tube in her stomach for feedings. Candy is doing better (and we thank God for that). We now have Candy home and only have to return to the clinic twice a week, then back in the hospital for three days every few weeks.

We would like to sincerely thank all of Candy's classmates, teachers and faculty from St. Clair High School, all the many different churches, businesses, family, friends, neighbors and co-workers from the whole community who have helped us

through this very difficult time. Please know how very grateful we are for all the prayers, telephone calls, visits, cards, flowers, gifts, donations and for the very successful blood drive. The blood drive was held by her classmates in honor of her 12th birthday. Twice the number of pints were received than what we were hoping for. Thanks also goes to *The Leeds News* and Kimberly Stark for the excellent article on the birthday blood

drive.

Thanks for showing your love for our Candy and being there for us when we needed a helping hand.

Mary, Bobby and Jason (Candy's big brother) Sparks
Odenville, Alabama

Editor's note: We don't normally run thank you letters like this. But if you read the story or know the family then you know that this is a very special case

Candy Sparks

Leeds News Editorial

anyone, suddenly said as that nurse exited the room, "Goodbye, nurse, don't let the door hit you where the Good Lord split you." We all just chuckled out loud.

Healing verse special delivery from God

July

We managed to escape for a few days from the hospital and went home. Going home, I began crying, and then hot tears traced their way down my cheeks and spilled over to my T-shirt. Bobby looked at me puzzled and asked, "What's wrong, Mom? We're going home. You should be happy."

I glanced over at our dainty little Candy sitting between us in our blue pickup truck, her big dimple shining and, as always, she is so delightful. "Overwhelming tears of joy," I answered.

Bubba met us at the car and scooped Candy up in his arms to carry her inside. She kissed him on his cheek as she put her arms around his neck.

Shortly after we got home, Ora Mae, our God-sent nurse and close friend came by. She was there to help us hook up all the pumps and monitors needed. We had to learn to do everything at home that they did for Candy in the hospital. Bobby had to put on sterile gloves to change Candy's central line bandage that was underneath her arm. Her central line held all the hook-up caps which connected to tubes leading into different pumps. We had to learn how to mix her medicines and food. We basically had to learn to be nurse, pharmacist and therapist. Ora Mae had agreed to come by on her way to work each day for lab samples and like clockwork she returned every afternoon on her way home to offer more help. What a God-sent nurse and angel we had in our Ora Mae.

That night after Ora Mae left, all four of us were totally exhausted. Candy couldn't walk so I slept by her side. That night after midnight Candy's alarm on her around-the-clock feeding pump went off. I reset the pump and then went to the restroom. Suddenly, I had an incredible urge to pick up my Bible. I never read my Bible. I often wondered why God just didn't excuse us from using the Bible. Didn't God realize that the Bible was old fashioned, from a different era, and very outdated? Suddenly, I looked down and felt my hand pick up the Bible. For some odd reason,

I started reading and immediately a verse seemed to jump out at me as if it were highlighted in gold.

I can do all things through Christ which strengtheneth me.

—Philippians 4:13

An incredible loving, peaceful feeling washed over me and I heard a voice in my head loud and clear commanding me, "Go tell Candy the verse." I obeyed.

I immediately went into Candy's room, woke her up and repeated the verse to her then added, "I don't know why Jesus instructed me to tell you that verse but he did." Through sleepy eyes she nodded her head, then she turned over and immediately went back to sleep. At 3:00 a.m., she woke me up crying uncontrollably but she didn't know why she was crying.

"Candy," I said, "remember the verse Jesus told me to tell you?" I repeated the verse to her:

I can do all things through Christ which strengtheneth me.

Again she nodded her head and went back to a peaceful sleep. At 8:00 the next morning I walked sleepy-eyed out to our mailbox. Today was my birthday and our wedding anniversary.

I hadn't even realized that until I opened the birthday card in the mail from Diane, one of my co-workers at BellSouth. When you go through such devastation and pain as we had you block out everything, focus only on keeping your daughter alive. Things had been so bad that at times I would actually forget to eat so it was no surprise that I had forgotten it was my birthday.

I tore open the envelope and read the card. I had to catch my breath. I couldn't believe my eyes.

My legs began running extremely fast. I tripped climbing up the steps going back into the house but nothing could have stopped me. With a sheepish grin all across my face, I rushed into the den and handed Candy the birthday card and then I asked her if she remembered the verse that Jesus had given her late last night. Her teary eyes got as big as saucers as she read aloud the verse my co-worker had handwritten at the bottom of that card.

I can do all things through Christ which strengtheneth me.

—Philippians 4:13

"You knew your friend was sending that card," Candy's always practical Dad replied in disbelief.

I responded with, "I had no idea. I didn't even know it was my birthday. Besides, Diane had to mail the card before midnight last night." How amazing was God's timing. That verse became our promise from God. We repeated it together night and day. I often reminded Candy the verse proclaimed all things. It didn't say all things except being able to walk again or being able to eat again. It promised that she could do all things through Christ.

As the days became months, sometimes Candy would want to give up. Trying to maneuver and get her in the bathtub without getting her central line wet was a challenge. She had all these tubes attached to her. Every step we took, her feeding pump and long pole had to go with us.

She couldn't walk, so she leaned on my shoulder for support or either strong Daddy or her Bubba would scoop her up in their arms rather than allow her to try to walk.

One night, tears streamed down Candy's face while she sat in the bathtub. She cried, "I just can't take it anymore. It's just not fair. Why me? Why did God do this to me?

My own tears seemed to bubble up inside as I dared not cry, but my tears flowed anyway. Fighting back my tears, I spoke and said with confidence, "Candy, remember the promise that God has given us? Hold God to it!"

So sincere, she asked, "Mom, can I really hold God to that?"

I explained to her, "By all means. That's exactly what God wants you to do. When you say that verse, all the angels in heaven will come down if necessary to be sure God's written word is carried out. Whatever you read in the Bible is pure and true. You can believe it with all your heart. God will not disappoint you."

From then on, Candy and I began a game each night. While she sat in the tub, we would find special verses in the Bible. With a yellow pencil we highlighted the verses that touched us. God began to talk to us through the yellow highlighted verses. It's amazing how many verses felt like warm hugs from God. I call them my candy kisses from God. Later in this book, I will tell you how those verses saved my daughter and brought her back from being dead for five minutes.

Powerful verses, awesome God!

It's OK to cry if you're in pain. Remember, tears are prayers, too. They travel to God when we can't speak.

Will our lives ever be back to normal?

For the first time since Candy got sick I had gone to buy groceries all by myself. I came back home crying so hard that Bobby couldn't figure out why I was so hysterical. My heart was like a too full dam and the walls of that dam were unable to hold it all in. I was guilt-ridden because Candy always went with me to buy groceries and I just couldn't handle the task without her. I couldn't seem to focus. I couldn't even remember how to count my money out to pay for the few groceries I had been able to somehow put in my buggy. My mind was just a fog, my nerves shot.

I remember leaving the grocery store shaking and in tears. I wondered what the little cashier clerk thought of me and I wondered if I our lives could ever be the same again.

I sat outside in my car crying, feeling sorry for myself and for my family. I missed the life we had before. It was taken from us in a blink of the eye. I loved working in corporate America dealing with the stress and demands of schedules and time frames. I had worked in that fast- paced life since I was sixteen. Now I couldn't even focus to buy groceries. This had taken a toll on our whole family. Jason had graduated high school and had to put his life on hold. Bobby and I had to sleep in separate beds so I could be next to Candy in her bed. Many times however, he joined us, sleeping in Candy's bed. I smiled to myself as I remembered sometimes there had even been all three of us sleeping in Candy's queen-size bed. Jason would often slide in there with us. As I drove home I had to keep blinking back the tears to see the road. When I got home I told Bobby I just can't do this without Candy beside me and I went to the den to be with her. She was joking and smiling as she and Jason played the game Clue. My little hero, I yearned for the day when her life would also be back to normal.

Our Journey

JOHN 11:25

August
through
December

Candy Sparks Fun Day

August

Talk about being smack-dab in the center of God's love, that's what Candy Sparks Fun Day was for us. Right in the middle of all our pain and suffering, our whole St. Clair County gave us a benefit day that outshines all other days. Candy had been so ill we didn't know if she would be physically able to attend this event. We were overwhelmed at all the preparation and planning that had been done to make this benefit day a reality. There were at least 85 or 95 businesses, organizations, churches, TV and radio stations sponsoring the day's events. Special thanks went out to Fox 6, NBC 13, Alabama 33/40, Rick and Bubba Radio Show, Classic Rock 99 and WASB. Our local Fire Department had a road block taking up donations. Every business, church or organization that owned a big road sign proudly displayed messages like "Candy Sparks benefit Sat. Aug 2nd at Odenville Baseball Field." The field was crowded with people of all ages. They shouted, waved flags and cheered when they saw our car approaching. We were so humbled. All of this was done out of love for Candy. Candy was so sick and looked so fragile as Jason carried her in his arms and placed her in a chair in the middle of all the excitement. Even though she couldn't walk, she insisted on wearing her brand new Nike tennis shoes. Her classmates were proud to stand beside her and they let her know they were her cheering squad showing their love and support for her. The whole day was just spectacular.

Businesses donated everything imaginable, even bikes for door prices and drawings. Candy Sparks Fun Day T-shirts were printed up and worn by about everyone. The winning team of the baseball tournament gave their trophy to Candy. There was a home run derby, pony rides, 4-wheeler rides, dunking machine and rubber ducky prize pools. They sold hamburgers, hot dogs, cold drinks. Clowns and balloons were there.

Love outpoured and running over for us was the only way to describe what we were in the middle of. Who were we that a community like this would come together to help us. Our family had always been on the other side of giving and helping. Now we were the ones in need and what an awesome town we live in that so many people would be there for us in so many different ways. We saw God that day face to face in all those people; joy unspeakable. Words cannot describe how humble and thankful and totally overwhelmed we were. There is no greater love than what we saw that day.

TV Anchor/Reporter Andrea Lindenburg was there with hugs and gifts for Candy. Andrea kept Candy's picture taped to her desk at work. Many times after that she came to visit Candy in the hospital. October of the following year, Andrea walked 26.2 miles in the Chicago Marathon in Candy's honor and crossed the finish line in six hours. We still have and treasure the "I'm going the distance for Candy" bracelet she wore in the marathon. While she was there in Chicago, Andrea bought Candy a pink TY Beanie Baby named Valentina. On one hospital visit, Andrea gave Candy her own personalized TV logo shirt that she herself had worn during TV coverage of a severe hurricane. "Just like I battled that storm out, you too are battling a severe storm in your own life and I know you will make it through it." That's what Andrea told Candy. What love, hope, strength and encouragement we found in Andrea. That support and love from Andrea continued way after Fun Day was over; in fact, for years Andrea was a big part of our lives.

The people in Odenville and the surrounding communities of Moody, Leeds, Branchville, Pell City, Ashville and Springville all feel they played a major role in Candy's surviving. She belongs to all of them. They all know and love her and they all did indeed play a big role in keeping her alive. **Candy represents answered prayers.** Those wonderful caring loving people sought God's face in deep, sincere, earnest prayers for Candy. Many people went to the altar to pray for Candy. They pleaded with God for Candy to survive. We were shown love that can't be measured. Churches from every denomination all around St. Clair County came together for the purpose of keeping Candy alive. We have been told that this was the first time that this many churches had joined hands for the same benefit. People we didn't even know were praying for Candy. Many came to our home asking if they could pray for her.

Special thanks to Laura, Tammy, Shirley, Pam and Judy who personally organized this awesome very successful love event. We can't imagine all the time and planning that went in to making this happen. Our hearts will always be full of love, respect and thankfulness for all that you have done for our family.

My grace is sufficient for thee; for my strength is made perfect in weakness.
—II Corinthians 12:9

Candy Sparks Fun Day T-shirt

Special Thanks to.

Andrea Lindenburg "FOX 6"
Alabama Coach Mike Dubose
Auburn Coach Terry Bowden
Atlanta Braves
Birmingham Barons
Alltel
National Cement Co.
Pepsi Cola
Golden Flake
Aamoco
Odenville Food Mart
Odenville Grocery
N.A.P.A.

St. Clair Senior Class '97
Laura's Cakes/Gloria's Arrang.
Ken Surles Taxidermy
Classic Rock 99
WQSB
Rick & Bubba 103.7
NBC 13
Alabama 33/40
Region's Bank
Chuck's
Mama D's Pizza
Western Auto
K Mart
Wal-Mart

Motion Industries
Head Start-Moody
Head Start-Pell City
Danny's Florist
Gaye's Barber Shop
Pop's Grocery
Jiff's B.B.Q
Dollar Greenhouses
The Open Book Store
Sandy's Gifts
Guadalajara
The Smart Shop
Sam's Grocery

K.J.'s
Thee Divine Assurance
Cracker Barrel
Quincey's
T.K & Mike
Heilig Meyers
Waffle House
Barbara's Clip 'N Curl
Pizza Hut
Shaw's BBQ
Jean's Flowers
Carlisle's BBQ
The Video Store
Taco Bell
Janice Wilson's Florist
Kay's Flowers

Special Thanks to.

O.Y.A.A.
for letting us use the ballpark and concession stand!

Lovejoy Realty
Conti-Brothers
Pleasant Valley Raceway
Mc Donald's
Subway
Merle Norman
Odenville Utility Bd.
Sam's Wholesale Club
Sheriff's Dept.
Shoal Bandits
Dorsett's Lawn Care
Abstream Raymote
Calvery

Ladies who baked cakes
Pants Store
Carl ANN Florist
B'ham Piston Warehouse
AmereX
Highland Bank
Rock Wool
Mineral Products
Drennen Walker
Central Club
Odenville Methodist Church
University of Alabama
Talladega Super Speedway
Pell City Baptist Church

Candy Sparks Fun Day Benefit
Thank You Posters

Signs from Candy's Fun Day

Moby Dick

Before Candy got sick, we had plans to build a new house on top of a magnificent hill overlooking our pasture at our farm which is about 15 minutes from our house. It was our life dream to live over there but something just wouldn't allow us to build.

No matter what we did, it just wouldn't come together. We had a builder, house plans and were ready. We had a very expensive road put in and what happened but a 100-year rain came and destroyed the road and culvert pipes, just washed it away. Old timers around said that kind of rain only comes once every 100 years. We reached road blocks on everything we did. It just wouldn't happen. At the time, we didn't understand why God kept throwing so many obstacles in our way. It seemed so unfair. What was God doing to us? Why wouldn't he allow us to build our new dream house? We are stubborn. We just kept trying different ways but, no matter how much we wanted it, we just couldn't have it.

Candy's Dad finally said, "Something is telling me **not** to build."

I agreed with him, "Let's listen to that something and wait until the time feels right."

Now, looking back, God very explicitly was telling us no. He knows what is ahead for us and how he intervenes in our behalf. After Candy got sick, we knew what that something was that just would not allow us to build.

When we were able to take a few days away from living in the hospital, we decided to take Candy to our farm for a peaceful afternoon. It had been a long time since we had been over there and we were really looking forward to being at our farm. Candy and Jason had always loved sitting on our little pier and fishing in one of our ponds. The sky was a calming light blue color (like my Candy's granddaddy's eyes) and just a slight breeze tickled our necks. All at once what looked like a little tiny tornado was circling in our little pond next to us. Candy took a step backwards, never taking her eyes off the circling notion. It kind of scared me and Candy until Dad assured us that it was only a water spout, which was totally amazing to watch. He explained that sometimes water spouts form over the ocean and can be dangerous to boats.

Candy noticed some tadpoles in the water. Her Dad scooped one up and put it in a bucket of water. Candy was all excited as we took it home. "Moby Dick is what I will call him" and so Moby Dick became a part of our family. We babied that tadpole and watched eagerly as he grew. Taking care and loving Moby Dick seemed to bring a renewed hope to Candy. We even took him in to meet the nurses on one of our trips to the clinic. After about six or seven weeks, Moby Dick had little legs starting to sprout. His head became more distinct and his body elongated. We fed him dead insects, plants and sometimes lettuce leaves. Candy wasn't able to be home very often but just knowing how Moby Dick was growing made her smile with pride like a new mother would with her new baby. We kept him in a fish bowl next to a neatly stacked pile of presents and cards that people had brought for Candy. One day while her Dad was home feeding Moby Dick, he noticed the tadpole's arms had begun to bulge and his arms popped out, elbows first. He was beginning to look like a teeny frog with a really long tail. To Dad's alarm, Moby Dick jumped out of his bowl and behind the presents. Dad knew how very much Candy adored that tadpole and had enjoyed watching it turn into a frog and, besides that, Moby Dick was now part of our family. Dad just couldn't leave him there to die so for about 30 minutes he wrestled with Moby Dick until finally he caught him and put him back in his bowl, this time with a top to cover it. Candy had tears tracking down her cheeks as she laughed with joy as Dad told her his story of finally catching Moby Dick.

By week 12, Moby Dick's tail was only a stub and he looked like a miniature version of an adult frog. Shortly after that, looking through blurring tears and a radiant smile on her face, Candy gave a farewell speech, then released her full grown adult Moby Dick into our pond at our farm.

Tears flowed freely then from Mom, Dad and Jason's faces. Our world had been turned upside down but Moby Dick had settled our world and it felt like a breath of fresh air and hope. Moby Dick had sprinkled our lives with lots of laughs and once in a while a tear or two.

"Dear Jesus, teach me to laugh; but don't let me forget I cried." Amen

A lady, whose name I do not remember, helped me find healing for my Candy

A lady whose name I do not remember came to our house from a church located in a different part of our St. Clair County. I don't even remember the name of the church. She said God had put in her heart to come to our house to pray for Candy. She asked if that was all right with me. What an uplifting thought, and I welcomed her into our house. I don't remember her name but I still treasure and use often the wrinkled up pages that hold the Bible verses and prayers that she had put together to help us. She had used white out and had handwritten Candy's name in each prayer. With her was her pastor.

They asked if they could lay hands on Candy and place a drop of oil on her forehead. Candy's eyes got all big and teary and it scared her. Remember she was just barely twelve years old and a tiny little thing. **As she cried, something totally amazing happened. She threw up a big hunk of what looked like a mass of flesh and it was as if that was what had closed up her esophagus**. Remember, the doctors had told us that Candy would probably never eat again by mouth because her esophagus had closed up. She had surgery to place a feeding tube directly into her stomach. The liquid food formula was pumped at slow motion to feed her. How we hated that pump and the feeding tube, but it saved her life. The doctor put her to sleep and did surgery every couple of weeks for esophageal dilatation. This had gone on for many months. The string that the doctors used to dilate her esophagus was left in and you could see it down Candy's face. Now as Candy choked, this strange bloody piece of flesh came flying out of her mouth. Immediately, within a few seconds after it happened, my phone rang.

I was still trying to figure out the situation. Our cousin, Michael, was on the phone and he insisted on talking with me immediately. Michael was a newly ordained minister working in prisons and had become my rock. I pulled much strength, courage and faith from Michael. Before I could tell him anything, he began giving praise to God and asking for me to tell him what had just happened. I was shocked at Michael's timing. As I told him he proclaimed, "I knew it, I knew it, I sensed something wonderful had just happened but didn't know what it was." With Michael on the phone I didn't have time to be afraid or to evaluate the situation because that phone call at the exact second I needed it was proof that what had just happened was a good thing. I'm still amazed at the timing of it all. God is very awesome.

The couple left while I was on the phone and I don't think I ever got the chance to thank them. They slipped away in the night. That night I began reading over and over again the list of prayers that the lady had so gently placed in my hand. What had taken place that night seemed to be what Candy had needed to get her healing started. Healing began to come to Candy as these powerful prayers actually seemed to come alive and become part of us.

If you are facing unbearable pain, hurt and fear and if all you have left seems to be fallen leaves and broken dreams, then try molding these prayers into your life. They worked for us.

Here are some of the precious treasures that this Godly woman had folded into my hand.

God, in accordance with Your Word...

I pray, O God, that because Jesus was wounded for Candy's transgressions and He was bruised for her iniquities, that by His stripes she is healed.

(Isaiah 53:5)

I pray, God, that You heal all Candy's diseases and redeem her life from destruction.

(Psalm 103:3-4)

I pray that Candy may prosper in all things and be in health, just as her soul prospers.

(3 John 1:2)

I pray that You will heal Candy, O Lord, and she shall be healed. Save her and she shall be saved.

(Jeremiah 17:14)

I pray, God, that You will restore health to Candy, and heal her wounds.

(Jeremiah 30:14)

I pray, O God, that Candy remembers that Jesus healed every sickness and every disease among the people.

(Matthew 9:35)

I pray, Jesus, that power goes out from You and heals Candy.

(Luke 6:10)

I pray, God, that I am not worthy that You should come under my roof. But only speak a word, and Candy will be healed.

(Matthew 8:8)

I pray that the prayer of faith will save Candy from her sickness and that You, Lord, will raise her up. And if she has committed sins, she will be forgiven.

(James 5:15)

I pray, God, that You give power to Candy who is weak, and that You increase her strength.

(Isaiah 40:29)

(Remember the doctors had told us that Candy may never walk again. For two years she couldn't walk and then after those two years she had to relearn how to walk through therapy. Because of that, the verses below have a very special place in my heart. I can attest to the fact that prayer works.)

I pray that Candy, shall wait on You, Lord and that she shall renew her strength. I pray that she shall mount up with wings like eagles, that she shall run and not be weary and that she shall walk and not faint.

(Isaiah 40:31)

I pray that You, Lord, are Candy's light and her salvation. Who shall she fear?

(Psalm 27:1)

I pray that Candy will fear not, for You are with her. I pray that she will be not dismayed for You are her God. You will strength her and help her and You will uphold her, with Your righteous right hand.

(Isaiah 41:10)

I pray that You, Lord, are Candy's rock and her fortress and her deliverer: her God, her strength, in whom she will trust: her shield and the horn of her salvation, her stronghold. I pray that she will call upon You, Lord, who are worthy to be praised: so shall she be saved from her enemies.

(Psalm 18:2-3)

I pray that Candy will be strong in You, Lord, and in the power of Your might. I pray that she will put on the whole armor of God, that she may be able to stand against the wiles of the devil. For she does not wrestle against flesh and blood, but against principalities, against powers, against the rulers of darkness of this age, against spiritual hosts of wickedness in the heavenly places.

(Ephesians 6:10-12)

I pray that Candy can do all things through Christ who strengthens her.

(Philippians 4:13)

I pray that You, God will grant Candy according to the riches of Your glory, to be strengthened with might through Your Spirit.

(Ephesians 3:16)

I pray, God, that You will strengthen Candy according to Your word.

(Psalm 119:28)

I pray that Candy will take up Your whole armor, God, that she may be able to withstand in the evil day, and having done all, to stand. I pray that she will stand therefore, having girded her waist with truth, having put on the breastplate of righteousness, and having shod her feet with the preparation of the gospel of peace: above all, taking the shield of faith with which she will be able to quench all the fiery darts of the wicked one. I pray also that she will take the helmet of salvation, and the sword of the Spirit, which is the word of God, praying always with all prayer and supplication in the Spirit.

(Ephesians 6:13-18)

I pray that Candy will be strengthened with all might, according to Your glorious power, God.

(Colossians 1:11)

I pray that Candy's Lord God, who goes before her, will fight for her.

(Deuteronomy 1:30)

I pray that if God is for Candy, who can be against her?

(Romans 8:31)

I pray that if Candy will indeed obey Your voice, God, and do all that You speak, then You will be an enemy to her enemies and an adversary to her adversaries.

(Exodus 23:22)

I pray that no weapon formed against Candy shall prosper and every tongue which rises against her in judgment, You, God, shall condemn.

(Isaiah 54:17)

I pray that You, Lord, are faithful, who will establish Candy and guard her from the evil one.

(2 Thessalonians 3:3)

I pray that Jesus has given Candy the authority to trample on serpents and scorpions, and over all the power of the enemy, and nothing shall by any means hurt her.

(Luke 10:19)

Let's join our faith and believe God for a miracle
Several people came to our house to pray for Candy. Several people went to the altar at their churches to pray. Help came to us in so many different ways. It was truly amazing.

Father God, we come to you in the name of Jesus. Father we come boldly before your throne asking for a miracle on behalf of Candy. We are standing in agreement for a complete turn around. We are decreeing and declaring total healing in her body. She will be able to walk again! She will be able to use all her limbs. Father, we know Satan meant this for bad, but you are going to revive her and give her a testimony to all. The doctors and nurses will be amazed at your mighty work in her life, Father God.

Now, Father, we ask that you give our family a peace that surpasses all understanding. Allow the angels to minister to our family and friends at this time. All these blessing we pray in your Son Jesus' name. AMEN!

Mr. Hall's lawnmower repairs

Talk about someone who could brighten any day with laughter. Being around Mr. Jim Hall felt like being smack-dab in the center of God's love. Mr. Hall lived across the street and took on the grandpa role for Candy and Jason. He's in heaven now with that little grin we loved so much and those eyes that twinkled like little flashlights were behind them. I think he loved to flash that grin because it made you wonder what he was up to or what he knew that no one else knew.

This is one of Mr. Hall's tall tales: One day while we were at work he went to his mailbox and spotted Bobby's beautiful delicious looking peppers growing around our mailbox. He decided to sneak a pepper when no one was looking. He loved the thrill of thinking he was getting away with something. (He really wasn't sneaking because we had told him to help himself.) He said he picked the prettiest colorful pepper, wiped it off with his hand, and popped it into mouth smiling at his success. At church the next Sunday, he confessed to having done this and he laughed, "That sucker was so hot, I spit it out. My mouth was on fire and I ran home for a cold glass of water. I guess that's what I got for stealing it." His laughter was contagious. It felt like warm sunshine wrapped around you.

Mr. Hall was always telling tall tales that would make your cheeks hurt from laughing so hard. Another day beside that same mailbox with the peppers wrapped around it, Mr. Hall spotted a snake sitting on the rock next to the mailbox. He said he ran home across the street got a rake and ran back over to beat the snake to death so it wouldn't bite us. Halfway through beating the snake to death he said he realized that it was a fake snake that Bobby had placed there to keep the birds away. I told him not to feel embarrassed because that same snake had caused a policeman distress. I walked outside one day and a policeman parked by our mailbox got out of his patrol car shouting at me, "Don't come any closer, stop right there, did you hear me? Stop right there." I froze, scared to death, wondering what in the world did this policeman think I had just done? Robbed a bank or killed someone? I held my arms over my head to surrender. Then the policeman pointed bravely at the snake. He was proud of himself for saving my life; however, that policeman left really quick, embarrassed when I confessed, "Oh, that's only a fake snake."

Another image floats around me as I remember one day when Mr. Hall's son, Jimmy, and his wife Myra walked across the street to see a very sick Candy. Years later, Jimmy would recall that day and what had tugged at his heart. Walking down our hallway, Jimmy had heard Candy talking with her dad. "Daddy, I want to and I'm trying with all my strength and my heart to walk, but I just can't make my legs move." Jimmy's eyes were drenched with tears. He says that day still lingers in his mind.

Well, back to Mr. Hall and his tall tales. Oh, how we loved that fellow. One day Mr. Hall appeared at our backdoor kind of shy, totally unlike him. He came inside and handled me a $50 bill and said he wanted to give it to us to use anyway we needed to while Candy was so sick. He said "Pay bills with it, buy groceries, whatever you need."

I tried to hand the money back to him, "Mr. Hall, we love you and we really appreciate this but you know we don't want to take your money. We're doing fine. Please take this money back."

Mr. Hall went on to say that his lawnmower had broken and the repair shop charged him $50 to fix it. I just knew then I had convinced him that the best thing would be to take that $50 and pay toward that lawnmower repair bill. We really didn't want to take his money.

He shuffled his feet a little, looked at me with no grin showing as he said, "You don't understand. God had told me to give you $50. I didn't listen to him so my lawnmower broke and it cost me $50 to fix it, so you have got to take this $50. You just have to. I can't afford for you not to take it." Then Mr. Hall flashed us that big smile of his and we saw the laughter in his eyes.

We miss Mr. Hall deep down in our hearts. He brought so much joy and laughter to our lives. We believe God has captured in his medicine bottle each of those tears we shed for Mr. Hall and God continues each day to pour those tears back out on our lives as laughter. If you hear laughter in the sky, that's our Mr. Jim Hall in heaven making the angels laugh out loud.

Count your blessings. God is in them. Mr. Hall was one of our greatest blessings from God.

Look at me. I'm riding a bicycle.

September

One of the many scary obstacles that we faced with Candy was her inability to move her lower limbs, so she was unable to walk for about two years. Then after two years she had to take therapy to learn to walk again. As Candy battled the deadly candida fungus infection her muscles became real weak and her bones were so fragile they told us she could break bones just by our turning or moving her in her bed. One month into her treatments she could no longer walk. Her lower limbs, especially her toes, would not move. We would massage those little legs and rub her little toes trying to persuade them to move. The doctors told us that Candy would probably never be able to walk again. That thought makes you have cold chills. The doctors put therapy boots on Candy so she wouldn't get blood clots in her little legs. Later in the treatment, the doctors had special braces made for Candy's legs to try to give her the ability to walk but she would never wear them. She also would not wear any of the adorable hats people had given us. Braces on her legs and hats to cover her little bald head just weren't Candy. She said she would rather just be herself.

Candy and I listened to what the doctors were telling us about her not being able to walk again, but our hearts were telling us that God had different plans. Day after day, Candy and I repeated her special verse that God had given us on my birthday and anniversary back in July. I kept reiterating to Candy that the verse said all things; that included walking. Candy and I believed in that verse. It was rooted deep down in our hearts.

I can do all things through Christ which strengtheneth me.

—Philippians 4:13

On this beautiful September day, as I looked outside, the dew sparkled, diamond-like tears of the early morning as it reflected the sun's love. What a magnificent day it was. Sounds of birds everywhere and the sweet scent of an early fall hung in the air. Candy asked to go outside and wanted to hold on to my shoulder with my arms around her waist and help her walk to the mailbox. Jason walked with us, giving Candy his strong arms for support. Jason's best friend, Trey Cobb, was with us on this postcard perfect day.

Outside, Candy spotted her bicycle and she said with confidence, "I want to ride my bike and have Bubba and Trey walk along side next to my bike. I can do it, Mom. If Bubba and Trey will stand beside me just in case I fall."

We all must have had a look of bewilderment on our faces as we said quietly, "Okay." Candy has always been like a breath of fresh air with her dynamic gusto for life. I watched Jason scoop Candy up and place her on the bike. Jason and Trey walked along beside her bike, holding their hands on the bike as Candy began to peddle. I stood by the mailbox watching and felt a hot tear race down my cheek. Candy didn't even realize that she had moved way ahead of the boys and was riding her bike all by herself. Trey and Jason looked at each other and gave thumbs up. Trey wiped the tears from his eyes with his sleeve. Up and down the road, Candy peddled, her sapphire and aqua blue T-shirt waving in the breeze. She rode and she rode and the more she rode the brighter that cute little dimple glowed. She told me later that it felt like God was nudging her on, telling her that she could do it. She wasn't able to walk, but there she was riding her bicycle up and down the road by herself with Jason, Trey and Mom standing far behind, amazed and very thankful.

At 5:30 p.m. when Candy's Dad came home, she couldn't wait to show him what she could do. As he came in the back door, Jason scooped Candy up in his arms, carried her out the front door and placed her on the bicycle seat. He walked with her to the road and waited beside her. I couldn't keep from grinning ear to ear as I coached Bobby into walking out on the front porch.

By then, Candy was riding the bike up and down the road, smiling and waving to her dad. Bobby's eyes watered. I know his mind must have been swimming against the current of the impossible. He seemed momentarily paralyzed and lost in thought. Then he leapt off the porch walking toward Candy. She giggled and increased her peddling as she continued to wave. She turned her bike around and headed back toward her Dad. He planted a kiss on her forehead and she put her head against his chest and her arms around his neck. Needless to say, that day we were all ecstatic with joy. Candy had taught us to expect great things from God. He sure delivered us blessings that day and we know that God's blessing bucket is really bottomless.

Sometimes we are so busy adding up our troubles that we forget to count our blessings.

Want God to talk to you?

Open a Bible. Hey, that's me saying that! I'm the one who always felt the Bible was outdated. I thought God should grant us pardon from reading it. How wrong I was! The Bible is solid gold. Open a Bible and soon God will point you toward verses that seem to jump out at you. Highlight the words with a yellow lead pencil or yellow highlighter. You will be amazed how

God will begin to talk to you through the Bible. Sometimes it may not be a whole verse, only part of a verse. The Bible is God's words. How wonderful that we can see with our eyes his written word and hold his written words in our hands. It's true, pure and it's going to happen. What peace, strength and answers you will find there. When God shows you his written word, you can believe it with all your heart, soul and mind. Hold God to his words.

For he shall give his angels charge over thee, to keep thee in all thy ways.

—Psalm 91:11

If your faith is strong and anchored down deep and you truly believe, then you can repeat God's written word aloud or silently to yourself. You can have total confidence that it will happen. I believe with all my heart that the angels in heaven will come down, if necessary, to make sure God's written word is carried out. Can you picture that scene in your mind? I do all the time. I visualize the angels in heaven hearing God's written word spoken by a believer and seeing angels rush down to earth to make sure it happens. Remember, it's not you telling God what to do. No one can tell God what to do. God is telling you what he will do. All you have to do is believe completely and give thanks. Do not waiver from your faith, even if it's new faith, as my faith was new. I visualize I'm holding tight to Jesus' hand. The Bible teaches that you can have complete confidence. Jesus is very faithful. What you read in the Bible is true and it's going to happen. Try talking to God on your knees. I promise you he will hear you.

"Lord, let's do lunch, just the two of us...we'll talk. Amen"

Our Journey

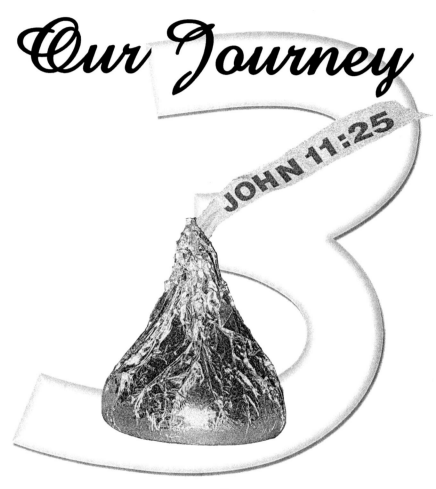

JOHN 11:25

Down
Memory
Lane

Down Memory Lane

As we end this chapter of our journey from April-December and before we plunge ahead to Candy Kisses' next year, let's take a trip down memory lane. It's a place where faraway visions of previous leaps of faith live in our minds and in our hearts. Yesterday is a sacred room in your heart where you keep your memories that you cherish. From your yesterdays you learn lessons and get encouragements to pass on to others. My heart is full of these floating thoughts and memories.

O ye of little faith

A tiny bit of background before I continue:

This chapter took place before Candy was born, many long years ago when her brother, Jason, was only two months old. This story, however, is an important part of my journey showing how God has been there directing our paths even before we knew who he was. My Mom, who was Candy and Jason's grandmother, is up in heaven now but I still sense her hugs.

Mom sensed I needed a hug when she greeted me at her front door. "What's wrong, Honey?" she asked.

Sadness and fear written all over my face I said, "Mom, I just came from the hospital. My Bobby is real sick. I told you how weak he had been for the last two weeks. He could hardly hold his head up so today I took him to the doctor. The doctor put him in a wheelchair and he wheeled him directly into the hospital himself. I'm afraid, Mom, so afraid." I explained the situation to Mom then headed home.

I left Mom's house feeling alone and helpless as I drove the forty-five minute drive back to my house. After retrieving my little two-month-old baby boy from my sister-in-law, MaryAnn, I headed home. As I lifted little Bobby Jason from his car seat, he snuggled close to me in the cool night air. Inside I sat in his Daddy's big black recliner and kissed my baby's forehead. His twinkling sky blue eyes were just like his Daddy's except tonight he looked at me as if he didn't understand why his Mommy's green eyes were liquid with tears. He looked up at me as if to say, "Don't cry, Mommy, I love you." How perfect life seemed in our little country house. *Why can't my Bobby be well and back home?* My mind raced with negative thoughts. I was scared and worried about my husband. He was so sick. I wondered if he would die. Life was so good. Finally I had found the love of my life, my soul mate. I had a wonderful job, a home full of love and a bundle of complete joy and happiness wrapped up in a blue blanket, my little son. I trembled at the thought of not having my hubby around. I was so in love with him and so dependent upon him. I couldn't imagine my life without him, yet I found myself feeling he was dying and there wasn't anything I could do to prevent that. What would little Jason and I do without his Daddy?

I held my baby close until he fell asleep then I placed him gently in his baby bed. I left the bathroom door open so I could keep an eye on my precious little boy as he slept. I knelt beside the bathroom sink and decided I would beg God to let Bobby live. Funny, but I had never talked with God while on my knees before, but I figured this was an emergency. I was in dire need. I was a Christian, saved at the very young tender age of 10. I grew up in church but I never felt very close to God. I knew he was there but I never read my Bible or even prayed much. In the back of my mind I thought God was real busy and much too important for me to bother him with my trivial problems, so I had gone through life without ever really talking to God.

Now I found myself on my knees hoping God wouldn't be too busy to hear me out. A thought seemed to jump into my head, *Do you remember when your life was in a mess and you didn't want to live? You cried out and prayed for someone just to love you.* I took a deep breath and thought to myself, *Wow, I haven't given it much thought before but maybe it had been God who gave me my Bobby in answer to that plea I had made years before.*

There on my knees, begging God to please allow Bobby to live, I suddenly felt a peace wash over me. The only way I can describe it is that it was like nothing I had ever experienced before. I had heard of people describing a presence that seemed to flood over them during a crisis. A warm feeling rushed from my toes to the top of my head. It felt so good. All of my senses seemed to be enhanced and heightened. It's kind of like when you take a bite of a delicious chocolate and your mind whispers, *Oh, heavenly.* I felt an oasis of tingling feelings. All at once I felt loved, relaxed, and enveloped in a warm peace that I never wanted to be separated from again. I heard a voice, loud and clear. It was the most powerful voice I had ever heard, so full of authority that it demanded attention, yet the voice was so beautiful that it was almost musical. Rolling thunder, that's how I'd have to describe the strong, crystal clear voice. Rolling thunder! I'll never forget the exact words. They seemed to reach deep down to my inner soul. The words were not rushed but spoken slowly, powerfully and lovingly. I wasn't afraid even though it sounded like rolling thunder!

"O ye of little faith! I love Bobby and I love you, Mary ... Bobby will be all right."

As quickly as the voice spoke, it seemed to disappear. I shuddered as a cool breeze seemed to drape over me. I felt cold and alone. Even though in my mind I thought, *Please don't leave me. Don't let that wonderful feeling be over,* I knew without a shadow of a doubt that Bobby would be okay. I knew he would not die. I didn't understand the enormous reality of what had just happened. In fact I got up from my knees, said a quick thank you, picked my baby up and went to bed. I slept peacefully with my little baby boy cradled next to me in our king-sized bed. When I awoke the next morning I noticed the rising sun reaching between the curtains and bathing the room.

The doctors kept Bobby in the hospital for two weeks till some of his strength began to return. They said he had some kind of inflammation of the brain, close to the spinal cord, and hinted that it may be caused from contact with a sick bird. Bobby's road to recovery was long. He had never missed a day's work but now found that he was too ill to work for more than four months. I never once doubted that he would recover.

O ye of little faith. Jesus spoke these same words to his disciples over 2000 years ago during a wild fierce storm. As the wind howled and the waves washed over the sides of the boat, Jesus slept. The disciples feared they would perish and woke Jesus up to rescue them. Jesus said to them, *"Why are ye fearful, O ye of little faith?"Then he arose, and rebuked the winds and the sea; and there was a great calm. But the men marveled, saying, "What manner of man is this, that even the winds and the sea obey him!"*

—Matthew 8:27-28

O ye of little faith. I did not realize the depth of those words that Jesus spoke to me when Bobby was so sick; Jesus' voice was as rolling thunder. Thirty something years later I am no longer *O ye of **little** faith*. I am now *O ye of **great** faith*.

Camp Smile-A-Mile Red Nose Day-How Ironic!

In the theater of my mind, I'm transported back in time to April Fool's Day 1991, "Red Nose Day." What a day of happiness, joy and celebration that had been.

Let me give you a little bit of background to bring you up to that "Red Nose Day" event.

In 1985, Camp Smile-A-Mile, a camp for children with cancer was born. My Candy Kisses was born that same year. In 1989 my best friend Cat and I were introduced to the camp known as Camp SAM. We were smitten with love for Camp Smile-A-Mile. Those little children with cancer wriggled their way into our hearts as Camp SAM became a big vital part of our lives. I was put on the Telephone Pioneer State Level representing Camp SAM. Cat, whom I fondly refer to as my "bestest friend" and my partner in crime was there backing me up. (Bestest is not a word but that is what we have always called each other.) She was the brains and I was the heart.

Soon Telephone Pioneers from all around the state fell in love with Camp SAM. With Camp SAM every child up to the age of eighteen who is a current or former cancer patient could go to camp. Qualified medical personnel from the Hematology-Oncology Department at Children's Hospital stay at the camp and administer chemotherapy as well as take care of all the first aid needs of the campers. That's where we first met our very loved and respected Dr. Berkow and Nurse Meredith who would end up being Candy's doctor and nurse some eight years later down the road called life.

On the first day of each camp session our Telephone Pioneers met the children at Children's Hospital. Cat, Jason, Candy and Cat's son Lance, I and several others were dressed as clowns as we walked all the children in lines to McDonald's located behind the hospital. The kids sang and danced their way across the street with clowns stopping the flow of traffic. Telephone Pioneers paid for each camper to have a happy meal which they proudly carried back with them on their return walk to the hospital. We gave them all goody bags and hugs before they boarded the rental buses that we had also paid for. The children rode buses while we drove behind them in cars. We sponsored forty children each year to attend camp. At the camp, other Telephone Pioneers members from around the state met us there to give the children a carnival. We had face painting, fishing booths, shaving cream battles, moon walks, crafts and etc. Our Pioneers had grills going with hot dogs, hamburgers and all the trimmings. Jason and Lance were ten years old and Candy was four when it all began. They made the cutest little clowns helping all the big clowns. What love they had for the little children who had cancer. Later in the week our Pioneers and their spouses would again join the children at camp for nighttime parties or dances. I have photo books filled from our Western cowboy dances, our costumes parties, our Hee Haw dances, and our Hawaii Aloha parties. Many times Jeff Cook of the country singing group "Alabama" was there at camp. He and his group "Alabama" were avid supporters of Camp SAM.

Camp SAM's newsletter soon proclaimed the Telephone Pioneers as their best friends. Quoting from their newsletter, "We were broke, not only broke, but in debt and without any reason for optimism. The Telephone Pioneers are the most involved friends we've ever had. Thank you for loving our kids." Over the years, here are some of the other things our Pioneers sponsored for Camp SAM. We paid for four busloads of Camp SAM kids and their siblings to go to Ft. Payne for the country singing group Alabama's big party. We also paid for lunches for everyone. We paid for T-shirts and printing. We set up WSAM, the camp radio station. Our Telephone Pioneers-sponsored clubs, the Gunwale Grabbers Canoe Club, the Pioneer Radio Club, the BellSouth Singers, and the Clown Corps helped provide many of the camp's activities. Through our cookbook sales we funded most of the cost for the new boys' dorm. We purchased the camp a white van and had their red monkey logo on the sides. Candy's daddy, Bobby, was on the board of directors for Camp SAM. The company Bobby worked for, Alltel, was also an avid supporter. They attended the camp events with us. Among the wonderful things that Alltel accomplished was to buy the camp a new golf cart, thus providing mobile transportation for the children at camp who had trouble walking or had even lost a limb to cancer. The golf cart had a dual purpose of transporting their trash to the big dumpster close to the road. The kids loved riding on that golf cart. It was always on the go, never parked very long.

The most talked about and remembered event that we gave to Camp SAM was our famous "Red Nose Day" established in 1991 by my best friend Cathy Kelley and me. It is still in existence some twenty one years later. Today many other events including auctions and relays are under the Red Nose label. I was elected President of the Telephone Pioneers for my South Council. Cat and I and several other Pioneers along with the Camp's Executive Director, Lynn Thompson went to visit Governor Guy Hunt in Montgomery in 1991. He signed a proclamation showing April 1st to be the official state "Red Nose Day" for Camp Smile-A-Mile. We have pictures and a framed certificate of the signing of that proclamation. Cat and I had traveled the state pulling in support for our "Red Nose Day" and Camp SAM. We attended several big conferences around the state to promote the camp video and to pull in supporters. Jeff Cook of the Alabama band

hosted our "Red Nose Day" commercial on television.
So April Fool's Day 1991 was a day for fun and
celebration. Businesses from around the state proudly
let their employees wear red noses. We literally sold
thousands of red noses at $1.00 each. All the
Telephone Pioneers around the whole state of
Alabama wore their own clown noses, and each
building had its own cake decorated with the words,
"Red Nose Day Telephone Pioneers Camp Smile-A-
Mile." We raised $28,000 the first year and $18,000
the second year to show our support and love for our
Camp Smile-A-Mile children. Now in 2012 Camp
Smile-A-Mile has more than 400 children and young
adults each year attending their camp events.

Can you imagine how my family and my best friend
Cat felt on April 1, 1997 when my very own precious
dainty little eleven-year-old daughter Candy was
diagnosed with leukemia?

I wanted to scream out to the world. *Hey, you have
the wrong person. There has to be some mistake. We are
avid supporters not campers. We council the parents of
children with cancer, we're on the other side of the fence.
Don't they know? Candy has been a clown at Camp Smile-
A-Mile. She was there to hug and comfort all the little ones
with cancer. This can't be happening to us. There has to be
some mistake. They can't try to tell us our child has leukemia.*

*How ironic, April 1st, April Fool's Day, Red Nose Day.
How ironic! The day that felt like a fist to the stomach, the
day our world fell apart and our lives were changed in a
blink of the eye. How ironic!*

God dwells in, around and through all things.

**Check out Camp Smile-A-Mile's website and
make a love donation to the camp. Tell them** *Candy
Kisses, My Miracle from God* **book sent you to them.
www.campsam.org**

Cat, Cousin Cliff, Mom and Candy supporting Camp SAM
TV's beloved kids star, Cousin Cliff Holman, died September 2008

Cross in the clouds

I open the bathroom curtains wide every morning in anticipation of the beautiful view of each fresh new day. I love to see how the day unfolds. At the end of the day, that's my favorite place to be as the sun sets. It's as if God paints the scene just for me. How can anyone look upon his magnificent creation and not know that God is real and that he loves us. I watch as the sun shines iridescent yellow, illumined by golden orange layers, deep navy and fiery reds. Each sunset is uniquely different and exciting.

The other day I saw a sunset painting at a hospital. It was beautifully painted but I thought it strange that the artist had chosen the color purple. I thought to myself, *That artist doesn't even know what a sunset looks like; everyone knows a sunset isn't purple.* Well, the next day looking out my bathroom window, I had to marvel in wonder as I viewed a painted sky of deep purple washed in threads of soft pink. It was phenomenal. The purple was so purple it was breathtaking. In my mind I could see Jesus smiling.

A few days later on a cold blistering January day, I noticed the sun was hidden and then reappeared in a beautiful sky of moving colors and pure white vapors. As the sun peeked through the fast moving clouds I saw a perfectly formed cross suddenly appear as if it had been placed there just for me. It was made out of clouds. Melancholy washed over me as I felt God's love. It felt like a warm hug. The cross was two-sided and perfectly straight from the top which seemed to drop from high out of the heavens to stand atop of my garage. It didn't linger there long but as I stood looking out my bathroom window I was intrigued at the wonder of it all.

I believe we value the beauty and the light more fully after we come through the darkness. I tell people that after our family went through the terrible ordeal of battling every day just to keep our little girl alive we see things differently now. I go outside and the colors are more vivid, more intense. I see beauty where I never saw beauty before.

I remember one afternoon last summer as my husband Bobby and I sat at an outdoor restaurant in Destin. We were oohing and aahing at the beauty of the sun setting on the water. As we watched the scene unfold, it was as if a big fiery orange ball slowly drifted down from the baby blue sky and came to rest upon the calm royal blue ocean. It was so beautiful it almost brought us to our knees. We looked around us at the crowded restaurant, all bars stools full of loud, laughing people enjoying life but who never even saw the beauty of the sunset, a sunset so dynamic and breathtaking. I feel full of awe, of wonder, at the love of God who surrounds us with a beautiful world and I can only imagine what he has in store in heaven for us.

Our Journey

JOHN 11:25

*January
through
June '98*

Thank you for going down memory lane with me. Let's continue on our Candy Kisses journey in faith. We have made it through this year, April to December, most of the time crawling but things are finally looking up for the Sparks family or so we thought . . .

Rock bottom and lower

January

All four of us (Daddy, Mom, Jason & Candy) sat on Candy's queen-size bed as Candy sang her favorite song "A Broken Wing" by Martina McBride. Charlotte from the physical therapy rehab center had given Candy that cassette for Christmas. Candy has a unique way of wiggling into everyone's heart. At the rehab center it was well known that country music was forbidden so what would Candy do but on each visit sneak over and put her tape in the machine. Candy sang that song using her whole body to imitate the video. All the therapists, office workers, customers and even the boss would applaud and laugh as she held the last long note then flash them all a big smile with that cute dimple shining. It's amazing how Candy wins over even the toughest of people and how they look forward to her brightening their day.

At home Candy had just delighted us with that same finale that she had performed for the rehab center when we heard a knock at our front door. Ora Mae, our God-sent nurse from Children's Hospital stood at our door with tears in her eyes. Sonya, one of Candy's dearest friends from the hospital had just lost her battle with leukemia and died at 1:15pm. We had to tell Candy but we never imagined the outcome would be so devastating.

Candy cried and said "I want my Bubba to hold me." Jason held her close. Her daddy and I joined in

on the hug. We all cried together. Candy asked
questions and made comments like

·   Am I next?

·   Why does God heal some and not others?

·   What will Sonya's Mom and Dad and her little
brother, Brandon, do without her?

I had only been back at work full time for two
weeks. At work the next day I wondered why Candy
hadn't called me or left me one of her famous singing
messages on my voice mail. I knew her heart was
broken and that she had cried all night long. When I
called home Jason had said that Candy had been
sick throwing up all morning. She didn't want to talk
with anyone and she wouldn't get out of bed. Through
her feeding tube in her stomach he tried to feed her
some formula. She threw it all up.

The next day I took a day's vacation to stay with
Candy. She had stopped throwing up and had even
been drinking some liquids. She was tired and wanted
to stay in bed. We still thought she was just depressed.
We began to worry when she asked her daddy if he
was leaving for work. It was 7:00 at night and he
leaves at 7:00 a.m. for work. She was confused, which
wasn't at all like Candy. When I tried to put her in
the bathtub she looked at me through glassy eyes.
She said, "I love you so much, Mom . . . everything is
going around, please make it stop. Go get my daddy. I
just want my daddy to hold me and love me. Go get
him quick." As her daddy carried her back to bed, she
said, "You are the best daddy in the entire world and
I love you so much. Just let me sleep. I will take a
bath tomorrow. I'll be okay tomorrow, I'm just so tired."

It was late when I called the nurse on call at the
clinic. She knew how we feared the emergency room
and since we had an appointment already for 8:00 the
next morning she first said it would be okay to wait
until tomorrow to bring Candy in. When I mentioned

that Candy wasn't real coherent, the nurse said she
would advise bringing Candy in. Candy cried and begged
us to wait until morning. She hated the emergency
room dilemma. We didn't know what to do. I called our
close family friend who lives a few houses from us.
Peggy works at a clinic and she is studying to be a
nurse. She rushed right over. After Peggy took Candy's
vital signs, she pulled me into another room and I
could see the look of fear in Peggy's eyes as she said,
"I don't want you to wait until morning. I want you to
take Candy in right now." She kept rushing us up as
we tried to pack an overnight bag. Peggy later told me
she was terrified and couldn't get us out of the house
fast enough. She didn't want to scare us but she said
she had never been so scared in her whole life. She
was so afraid for Candy. Later Peggy would say that
she had always questioned what her purpose is life
really was. After that night, she knew that her purpose
in life was to be there to save Candy's life.

Jason carried Candy into the emergency waiting
room. Her blood pressure registered 20/20. Normal
for her was somewhere around 120/70. They said
their machine must be messed up. It was a relief to
be greeted and ushered back in the emergency room
by a resident doctor who we were fond of. She had
treated Candy when she was so sick months before.
After they took Candy's blood work and sent it to the
lab they came back in and said, "The lab messed up
big time on the results so we need another blood
sample." They started giving Candy fluids at a high
speed. They came back in again and took Candy's
blood a third time but this time from a needle in her
arm rather than from her central line. They said for
some reason the lab work from her line wasn't
accurate. All of her electrolytes seemed shuffled
around. For example they said the first lab had her
sugar as 1000 and the second had 500. The normal

range was 70-110. All the readings were impossible. They said Candy wouldn't be alive with the results that the previous two blood tests showed and these new results would be more adequate. After Candy received intravenous fluid she seemed to revive and we figured we would go home soon. How shocked we were when they came rushing back in and said Candy was going to Intensive Care. What a sickening feeling we all had because we knew how scared Candy was.

It just didn't add up. Candy was acting fine again and we couldn't figure out why we couldn't just go up to a regular room on the fifth floor where all our special nurses were. The Intensive Care doctor told us Candy was the sickest child in the whole Intensive Care unit. How obscure! She didn't even act sick. They wanted to start antibiotics immediately and I argued with them. I explained that the deadly candida fungus infection Candy had before was caused from socking the antibiotics to her and since then antibiotics were a no no. What if they caused all that to come back again, how devastating. I made them call one of our doctors on call at his home. When I talked with the doctor myself he said, "Mrs. Sparks, this is not the time to beat the emergency doctors up. This is the time to let the doctors do whatever is necessary to save Candy's life."

I kissed Candy and left her daddy and brother to stay with her while I made a phone call to her Aunt Ann. Candy wasn't connected to any monitors, yet but I noticed the nurses pulling all the equipment into the room as I walked into the hall. We had been at the hospital for less than 30 minutes. The waiting room outside ICU had people asleep everywhere. Some Moms and Dads camped out on mats with pillows and blankets, others curled up in chairs and some under the chairs in every corner of the room. Some were asleep, some wide awake as if in a daze, some reading

Bibles. I felt their pain as much as my own. I tried to make a phone call but froze when Jason and Bobby burst through the waiting room door shouting, "Candy is dead! She's dead!"

The words freeze in the air. I turn to see the look of fear in everyone's eyes in the waiting room. No one is asleep now. I drop the telephone receiver to the ground and leave it hanging. My feet feel heavy and glued to the floor. I feel my husband grab my arm and we run. Running feels as if we are floating. I need to run through the ICU doors to get to my little girl. She can't be dead. I must do something. I need to get to her. We ran into the hall. Right in front of the ICU swinging doors Jason fell to the floor and sat with his back against the wall. In slow motion I watch as my husband slides down the wall beside Jason and he lands in a sitting position, as if in shock.

Bobby's and Jason's faces were pale with blank looks and tears streaming down their cheeks. I started to run through the swinging doors of the ICU but Jason held me back saying, "Please, Mom, don't go in there. Please, please don't go in there."

I yelled, "No! No! There has to be some mistake. God told me he was healing Candy. He promised me. He also told Candy he was healing her."

Bobby looked like he was close to a heart attack. He could hardly breathe and he clearly wanted to die too. He said, "You're wrong. Did God lie to you, Mary. I saw her die. I'll never forget that look as long as I live. That look will haunt me the rest of my life. She's dead; we saw her die." Bobby didn't say that to be disloyal to God but he said it because he was in shock and needed me to face reality.

I turned again to Jason knowing he would tell me something different. I expected him to say that his daddy was mistaken. Instead Jason whispered through his tears, "I was there Mom. I saw it too.

Candy is gone." Jason's heart was broken into a thousand pieces. When Jason was little he always begged for a baby sister named Candy. He loved his sister so very much.

I refused to accept reality. "No! I'm not wrong and God doesn't lie," I proclaimed with confidence that I didn't know I had until then. "He promised me! God promised Candy! I'm holding God to his promise. I refuse to accept this. Total healing is what he promised and I won't accept anything less. I'm holding God to his promise."

Bobby looked at me with all hope gone from his eyes. He just shook his head in disbelief. I dropped to my knees and began praying out loud. I heard myself shout out loud, "*No.*" The word no seemed to remain in my throat and echoes out to the walls. "God promised me he was healing Candy."

I got up from my knees and looked through the tiny glass window on the ICU swinging doors.

I see doctors and nurses running around in high speed putting their emergency training and expertise in high gear. You can feel their adrenaline rush being pumped up as they ever so hurriedly connect Candy to all kinds of machines. A big tall doctor was putting electric shocks onto Candy's chest. No more slow motion. This scene is in fast forward. I watched in horror. I see my dainty little 12-year-old daughter, Candy, her body still and lifeless and then I realized they are trying to revive her. I felt like I was watching an emergency room drama unfold before my eyes, just like on TV. I watched as her tiny body seemed to lift itself up from the bed and fall back down. I dropped back to my knees to talk to God again.

Suddenly I remembered the Bible verse that I had taped to my bathroom mirror. I had crossed out the word she and in red replaced it with Candy. I had repeated that verse hundreds of times each day until it was embedded in my mind and in my heart. I felt it was God's promise to me. All at once I remembered that promise loud and clear:

...Fear not: believe only, and she [Candy] shall be made whole [well].
—Luke 8:50

I got up again from my knees and looked through the tiny window. This time I saw beyond the doctors and nurses, beyond Candy's small body that had just again ballooned upward from the latest shock treatment as they tried to force her heart back to beating. An eternity passed and then a nurse came through the swinging doors. She flashed us an exhausted smile, a smile of relief. "We have a heartbeat and Candy is connected to a life support breathing machine to give her heart a rest." It was documented that Candy was gone between three and five minutes in cardiac arrest. From what we saw it was at least five minutes. The nurse helped me pry Bobby and Jason loose from the wall and she ushered us into a private room. We counted twenty doctors going in the conference room in front of us to discuss what had just happened to Candy and why. The doctors were completely stunned. Candy had been at the clinic just a few days before and her lab work had shown everything was okay.

The results from the very first tests had been accurate. Their machines had not been malfunctioning. Her blood pressure had been 20/20, her sugar 1000 and all her electrolytes were indeed scrambled and unreadable, any one of which could have killed her. Common electrolytes that are measured by doctors through blood testing include sodium, potassium, chloride, and bicarbonate. I said a prayer of thanks for Peggy, who had insisted that we rush to the hospital that night instead of waiting until morning. Thank God Peggy was in the right place at the right time and had the knowledge to read Candy's vital signs and the forcefulness to rush us out without even time to pack a bag.

It would be forty-eight hours until we knew anything, and the doctors couldn't tell us for sure for two weeks if Candy would live or die. I already knew the answer to that question. I held on to God's promise. I knew if I let go for just a second that Candy would be gone. The hospital allowed us to stay the rest of that night in that private meeting room. Bobby lay on the couch with his hands covering his eyes. Jason sat in a chair with his Nike hat low over his face. I was on my knees by a small table praying out loud. I held on strong and that night I found the meaning of true faith.

I turned to face Bobby. My heart ached so very much for all three of us. Pain unimaginable filled the room. Emptiness and helplessness was felt all around. Our burden was so heavy. Bobby appeared in shock and didn't want to talk about it but I needed to know what had happened, what had gone wrong. I saw Jason's tear-streaked face as he slid further down in his chair and covered his face even more.

"I thought the fluids were reviving her. I thought she would be okay then," Bobby whispered and then continued. "She looked at me, worry and fear showing on her face. I could tell she didn't want to cause us any pain. I wanted to help her but I couldn't do anything. Her eyes wide and fearful, she seemed more worried about us than for herself. We each held her hand but the nurses pushed us aside. Suddenly she got a strange look on her face like, 'I know something that you don't know.' Then she said, 'Come play with me.' I thought I heard her call out to Sonya. It sounded like Sonya's name then Candy said, Hula hoops . . .

blue . . . trampoline . . sky . . ."

Bobby looked puzzled and continued talking with a blank expression on his face "She sat up then..... threw up violently and all this green stuff gushed forth out of her mouth and nose. Her eyes still open looked weird and her little head fell to the side. I saw it, Mary. That image will haunt me for the rest of my life. I saw her die. Then I heard the nurses scream for more help. The doctors and nurses started rushing in and we were pushed out the door. Jason and I ran to find you." All his energy drained and hot tears flowing down his cheeks Bobby lay back down on the couch lifeless.

I cried out loud, "But thank God, she is back. She's going to make it." Then I hit the floor again on my knees praying out loud by the night stand.

I must tell Jesus. I must tell Jesus. I cannot bear this burden alone!

It was about 2:00 a.m. I managed to make three telephone calls. It was the middle of the night, a very long drive to the hospital yet our family, friends and my pastor, Brother Norman, seemed to walk in within minutes. My friend, Cat, held me close. I kept reiterating to them that God had told me he was healing Candy and that I'm holding God to it. I wouldn't accept anything else. My sister Evelyn hugged me and she said, "I never knew you had such strong faith." Truth was my strong faith was very new.

My brother-in-law Ralph pulled me out in the hall and said to me, ***"Mary, if God told you he was healing Candy, then you hold on to that. Don't let anyone tell you different. Don't believe what you see with your own eyes. Hold on to that promise with all your heart and strength, with everything that you are made of."*** My brother-in-law himself had recently suffered the great grief of losing his own son, Dallas, 21 years old, who had been killed by a drunk driver. Still Ralph knew of God's amazing grace. I held steadfast to God's promise.

A lady whom I had never seen before came to our conference room doorway and asked to have a minute with me. I didn't know who she was or how she had heard what we were going through. She hugged me and said, "I won't keep you but a minute. I just wanted to see in person the Mom who was going on faith alone to keep her daughter alive. A Mom who was holding tight to the promise of God's word. God bless you." Then she disappeared.

I kept reminding Jesus that he had promised to heal Candy. I told him I was holding him to his word. ***You can't delegate to God and you certainly can't tell God what to do. You can, however, hold God to what he has told you and know it is true. God wants you to do that.*** He won't disappoint you. God is very faithful and powerful. I wasn't trying to make God do something. God had already told me what he would do. I just held on to that truth. I can attest to the fact that no matter what the situation around you looks like, no matter what you physically see with your own eyes, no matter how hopeless things appear, you can hold on to Jesus' hand. You can know without a shadow of a doubt that what you see is not final. What could be more final or more hopeless than death? I held on tight with everything I had. I refused to let go. I refused to believe anything other than God's word. I believe with all my heart and soul that if I had wavered from my faith for just a second I would have lost Candy. I had to refuse to let go. I had to hold God to his word and believe with all my heart that he would make good on his promise.

When you do what you can, God will do what

you can't.

ICU waiting room wise father's advice

It was the day after Candy had died for five minutes and they had shocked her heart back to beating that I was completely worn out. I slumped down in a chair in the ICU waiting room. I recognized a dad that had a young son in the ICU. During those times you form a special bond with the others around you that also have pain written all over their faces. The dad folded the Bible he was reading and sat down in the chair next to me. I was familiar with the story of his son who had many times been in the Children's Hospital ICU over the last few years. He shared something with me that was so powerful that I found strength in his words.

Here's what he told me. I will never forget his wise words.

"To survive ICU you need to walk by faith and not sight and I'll tell you how to do that. It's simple. Look beyond the ICU; look all the way through it to the other side. There you will see Jesus with his arms stretched out wide. You need to picture your daughter all well and healed. You need to keep reminding yourself that what you see in the ICU is not real. All the life support machines, all the wires, pumps and monitors, everything is not real. Don't focus on all that. Don't let the devil keep you from focusing on Jesus by believing what your eyes see. Learn to see with your heart. What you see with your heart is real. The ICU is not real. Learn to see Candy past all of this, healthy and strong. You can make it through this. Walk by faith not sight."

I actually became very good at practicing what this man taught me. Each time I walked through the ICU doors during the restricted time that we were allowed in I would think to myself, *this is not real.* I imagined the ICU being a big box that I could actually see all the way through. My eyes learned to focus on Jesus on the outward side of the box. I could see him with his arms stretched out wide. Let me tell you I soon began not walking to Jesus but running to him. Every thought of the ICU in my mind soon became unreal. I wouldn't accept my Candy broken. I saw her all well and healed, even walking. The doctors and nurses had told me she might never walk again but I saw her not only walking but running. It was two weeks in the ICU before the doctors would tell me if Candy would survive. They said even if she did live she probably would have brain damage. I already knew how things would turn out. I had no doubts or fears. My heart had taught me to walk by faith not by sight. God healed my young daughter. Even the doctors and nurses were elated to proclaim that my Candy is truly a miracle from God.

Now faith is being sure of what we hope for and certain of what we do not see.
—Hebrews 11:1

Prayer asks for rain; faith brings the umbrella.

Couch baked potato

Candy was on a life support ventilator and in critical condition in the ICU for two weeks. She had an assigned nurse who sat by her side every moment of the day and night. She was way too sick to say her favorite verse so I whispered it constantly in her ear. At first she didn't respond at all but evidently she got to where she would just nod her head in agreement to let me know she had heard me as I reiterated over and over, *"I can do all things through Christ which strengtheneth me."*

The doctors had warned us that Candy might very

well have brain damage because she had been dead for so long. Candy had not shown very much movement but one day while her daddy and I waited by her ICU bed to talk with the doctors Candy raised her sick head, opened her eyes wide, looked up at the silent television screen high over the foot of her bed, and then she looked directly at us and said, "Couch baked potato." Her daddy and I looked at each other and worried that Candy wasn't coherent. I saw the fear in her Daddy's eyes questioning if Candy had brain damage. We must have looked real puzzled. We thought she was sound asleep. Little fragile Candy again said "couch baked potato" and pointed her little finger at the silent television screen. Then she quickly turned back over and drifted back into a deep peaceful sleep cradling her pillow pal, Oink.

What a rush of thankfulness we felt seeing the Wheel of Fortune Game on television with only two letters filled in. We were elated with joy. Candy had solved the puzzle and was telling us the answer. Brain damage, we knew then absolutely was not there because our Candy Kisses was back and as smart as ever. Thank God! He always finds a way to give us warm hugs.

The doctors and nurses told us they knew Candy's healing hadn't come totally from them or from the medicines. They knew someone much higher had to be in control. They had all prayed for her. Everyone began calling Candy a miracle. One of our favorite nurses from earlier in the summer visited us during ICU and she said Candy had twelve lives and had only used up three of them.

One of the hospital chaplains told us that Candy had more church pastors stopping by his office checking on her than anyone had ever had before. He said the pastors and ministers came from many different types of churches. He jokingly said to us, "I know that God is hearing the name of Candy so much that I believe every time he hears the word Candy he automatically says 'Sparks'?"

Only Ice

Candy was so thirsty and while in ICU they would not allow her to drink anything by mouth. My mind journeyed back to painful memories of the previous year when she had also been restricted from drinking anything. Back then it was because of her sodium count being low. Most children had problems with high sodium counts. But with Candy everything was different than the norm. Whatever the doctors expected went the opposite way for Candy. That's why they had to rewrite the books for her. She made the doctors rethink everything though in a different direction. Her body reaction to every crisis was different from other children. Because she had a hole in her heart the sodium electrolyte being low was especially dangerous so back then liquid by mouth was restricted until her sodium count increased to a safe level. Other kids had to drink lots of fluids but with Candy's low sodium count they didn't want her to drink anything. Candy would play by the rules for only so long then she would sneak to the sink and put her head under the facet and drink just a tiny sip of water when she thought no one was looking.

With this new crisis of being back in the ICU, the doctors had wanted to give her heart and pancreas a rest so they once again had restricted her from drinking anything. The only thing she could have was ice and we had to feed it via her spoon one little cube at a time. She was only allowed two or three little tiny cubes every few hours. Candy was beginning to recover so one day a young doctor intern had mistakenly asked Candy what she would like to drink.

Candy with her cute little grin and innocent face had persuaded him that a Sprite would work fine. He disappeared but came back real soon with the iced down Sprite in a paper cup. Just as he started to pass the cup to her a nurse entered the room frowning and shouting "No way! She can't have liquids." It was like I was watching a chase scene from television. Quick thinking little Candy wouldn't be outdone so she grabbed the paper cup from the young man's hand and proceeded to guzzle the Sprite down before the nurse could pry it from her hand.

The whole time the nurse was quietly moaning, "The doctor will be so mad. I can't believe you gave her liquids." The young doctor intern seemed to throw Candy a grin and I saw her wink at him as she was grinning ear to ear.

A cop's blue light flashing

Late one afternoon while Candy was still in the ICU, I had to go home to get some clean clothes. Bobby and Jason stayed with Candy. It was after dark and I pulled to the side of the road as a cop's blue light beckoned me over. I shivered as I thought, "What else can happen? What else can go wrong?" I squeezed my eyes closed for a brief second and tried to rid my mind of the images parading across it of my Candy so very sick asleep in her hospital bed. It's funny how you remember people who are so kind to you when your heart hurts so much. They seem to hurt for you and with you. I have always felt people's pain that way.

You also remember those few who are so busy with their life pace that they seem to enjoy other's pain. That cop gave me a ticket for having one headlight out. I guess I had a quiver in my voice as I told him of my situation of having a child in intensive care on life support. My car hardly ever left the hospital parking deck but I promised to get the headlight fixed soon. He told me he had better not even see me driving back to the hospital later that night unless my headlight was fixed and threatened me with a bigger fine and possibly facing the judge. I begged, "Can't you give me a couple of days? You can check with the hospital if you don't believe me. I have to get back to the hospital in a few hours." My emotions swelled and tears misted my eyes but knowing I would be driving back that same way going back to the hospital I made myself pull in a service station and paid them to put a new headlight in my car before I went on my way home. I have never forgotten that cop. My thoughts were still a jumbled mess and my exhausted mind refused to relax so rather than take a nap I headed back to the hospital.

This chapter is dedicated to the memory of

Sonya Terrell

On this journey there were two precious beautiful
young girls.
Their story and their testimony forever linked
together.
Their friendship and love for each other is eternal.
They shared their dreams and secrets.
One girl twelve and the other girl sixteen.
Both girls battled leukemia and also battled the
very serious candidiasis infection;
Same hospital; rooms next to each other.
Both girls have a brother; one has an older brother,
one has a younger brother.
Each girl truly loves her own brother: the light of
her life.
Both girls are known as "Daddy's Little Girl;
Daddy's Whole World"
One girl made it to live.
One girl made it to heaven.
One girl touching and changing lives from here on
earth.
One girl touching and influencing lives from
heaven.
Both girls are truly miracles from a loving heavenly
Father.
Each girl's mother has found peace, comfort and
strength from God.

Candy's friend Sonya

Special Angel Sonya goes to heaven

Candy had a very special friend from the hospital named Sonya. Their paths crossed almost every day. Sonya's story is totally amazing. I think you will agree:

Scarlet remembers well the day Sonya, her precious teenage daughter, was diagnosed with leukemia and how the silence that followed seemed to echo off the walls: Glassy-eyed, we tried to say what we were feeling but found that the words wouldn't come out. We tried to be brave but actually Sonya was the brave one. Our little hero only fifteen years old said, ***"Please Mother and Daddy don't worry. God will take care of me."*** Her faith in God filled our hearts. Our eyes overflowed with burning tears as the doctor asked if we had any questions. For us so many unanswered, afraid-to-ask questions flooded our minds. We didn't know what to say but we heard Sonya say, "Doctor, there is one thing I want you to do for me; make sure I can still go on the teen retreat to Camp Sonrise this summer. Our church sends us teens to camp and it is my favorite place in the entire world."

Shaking his head yes the doctor replied,

Sonya and her Mom, Scarlet

"Absolutely, that will be our game plan." Sonya threw her dad that grin that had always made him feel as if he had just won a marathon. I planted a kiss on my daughter's forehead. I knew that Camp Sonrise was where she had accepted Jesus as her Savior only a few years earlier. As the days became months and summer arrived, Sonya was able to attend three out of the five days at Camp Sonrise. She was elated with happiness to get to see all her friends.

In the midst of all our pain and heartache, God surrounded us with the beauty of his creation.

Love poured out and overflowed from Sonya's fellow classmates, family, friends, neighbors, coworkers and from our church. Whispered hopes, beautiful sunsets and breathtaking rainbows all helped ease our heavy hearts. Somehow we just wanted to crawl out of our pain. It was like a cluster of low black-bellied clouds hung over our heads and occasionally the sun would break through. We soon learned that when all you have is God, you have all you need.

**Sonya's receives a new shiny red sportscar
for her 16th birthday**

****

Sonya and Candy became good friends, almost roommates. Their rooms were next to each other. They shared the same nurses. When the nurses came in, each girl would inquire about the health of the other. Days became weeks and weeks became months. Both families seemed to literally live in the hospital. We parents would sometimes share tears and heartaches over lunch.

The hospital had special activities for their young patients. There was a special room on the fifth floor where they could make crafts, paint pictures or play video games. It was a fun get-away room for the kids. Many days, one of the two girls would be too sick to go but several times the two of them met together in that special room. The days were long and sleep rarely came for us. I remember well how each girl would sneak a peek in the other one's room just to throw her pal a smile each time she walked passed her door. How we loved our special friend Sonya. She had such a gusto for life. It just made you feel good to be around her, like a warm hug. She had that "can't keep me down attitude." She was always smiling and her laughter bounced off the walls.

In July, Sonya and her mother Scarlet stood smiling in the doorway of Candy's hospital room. We were always kidding with Sonya about how much she reminded us of the young country singer, LeAnn Rimes. Today Sonya had her short bouncy beautiful blond wig on and she dramatically announced her triumph. "Guess what? I'm going home. My six months of chemo treatments are over. I'm still in remission and now officially in maintenance." Giggling with that ray of sunshine all around her, she sat down next to Candy. Our nurse Lisa sat on the opposite edge of Candy's bed. Lisa was young and wasn't much bigger than Candy. On her head she wore a baseball cap turned backwards as she chatted with the girls. Candy, Sonya and Lisa were all joined at the hips. They made such a good team. The girls talked with Lisa, trusted her like she was their big sister. Candy had turned twelve in May and Sonya would soon be sixteen. Sonya had made plans with Candy that when she got her driver's license they would go out riding and looking for boys. Sonya was excited about going back to finish high school and putting her life back together. The three of them all laughed and carried on. They shared their secrets and dreams for the future. Sonya hugged Candy tight and kissed her on the top of her head as she said, "Can Can, I wish you could get out of this place like I am." Then all three of them gathered in a big group hug. Bobby hugged Sonya at the door. "I'm proud of you kid. However, I don't want to see you back in this hospital again, only in the clinic for checkups. You go out there, have fun, enjoy life and live things up but take good care of yourself."

I added, "You're so special to us."

A few weeks later, Sonya, wearing her pretty blond wig stood again at our same hospital room doorway. This time her dad Robert, elated with happiness, stood next to her. Sonya looked so good and she was glowing from the inside out. It made our hearts feel so good to see how wonderful she looked. She announced, "I just had a birthday. I'm sixteen with a brand new red shiny car. I'm back in school and, Candy, remember that you and I are going cruising for boys as soon as you get well enough." Candy grinned from ear to ear and gave Sonya a thumbs up. Sonya's 16th birthday celebrated her triumph and victory. She was on her way to a new life. We were all so proud for her and her family.

September came and we ourselves got to go home from the hospital for a little while.

One day at home I was so down in the dumps.

Sonya's mother brightened up my hopeless day with her call that night. She loved us and wanted to be sure we were okay. I remember that Scarlet said she felt that the entire trauma they had lived through with Sonya being so sick was nothing compared to what she knew we had endured with Candy. (How little did we know that later down the road of life their trauma and loss would end up far exceeding ours.) Scarlet was so compassionate talking with me. I'm thoroughly convinced that God loves us, encourages us, nurtures us, and supports us through other caring people. Sonya's mom Scarlet is one of those special people.

As Scarlet and I chatted my heart sank as I heard her say, "The doctors are looking for a bone marrow donor for Sonya. She's doing great, thank God, but the type of leukemia Sonya has usually comes back. To be on the safe side they want a donor available. Scarlet went on to say that the Albertville Fire Department where Sonya's dad, Robert worked had sponsored a blood drive/donor drive. The whole community rolled up their sleeves to help find the perfect donor match. Her voice was now filled with emotion and I could picture a waterfall of tears rolling down her cheeks. "No donor match was found." My heart hurt for her. Their church had been there supporting them with prayers, love, visits and donations. Scarlet and Robert were so grateful for all the love poured out, overflowing on them, by so many different people who lovingly carried them on their shoulders each day.

Friends are like rainbows. They brighten your life when a storm seems to envelope you.

Later we heard from our fifth floor nurses that no one had realized that Sonya was sick again until her blood work in the clinic indicated low white blood cells and a low platelet count. Sonya was readmitted to the hospital on November 1st. Sonya's leukemia was back. Severe, very aggressive chemo had to be restarted. A perfect match bone marrow donor had been found and was alerted to be ready in about six weeks. Christmas Day, Sonya was allowed to leave the hospital and go to her parents rented apartment close to Children's Hospital for a few hours.

After Christmas, every Wednesday when Candy came to the clinic she would rush up to the fifth floor to visit Sonya who was still in the hospital. Our special fifth floor nurse, Lisa, and Candy would embrace in a hug and have a cry for Sonya after each visit. Sonya soon developed the same deadly fungal candidiasis infection that Candy had struggled with for nine months. We knew that most people who get that cruel infection die within a week. Candy had defied the odds but Sonya lost her battle in less than one week. Sonya died on January 18. The trauma of Sonya's death was what broke Candy's heart, causing her to go rock bottom and two days later die herself for those five minutes. Candy had wanted to give up. She didn't want to live without Sonya.

Roger, one of our male nurses that Candy and Sonya had adored, also felt like giving up and quitting his nursing career. While Candy was still in intensive care battling for her life I saw Roger in the cafeteria. He said it just wasn't worth it anymore after losing Sonya. Then another child had died the day after Sonya. Roger's eyes were filled with tears as he said, "And now look what is happening to Candy. I just don't think it's worth it. I'm not cut out to be a nurse."

I pleaded with Roger, "When you see Candy you will know what you do is all worth it. Candy is our miracle from God. The ICU doctors are amazed at how Candy is bouncing back. When we get to go back to the fifth floor Candy will need you even more than before."

Candy had always tugged at Roger's heart anyway. When she did something that would make Roger proud of her she would flash him that big smile and ask of him "Roger, who's the man now?"

Roger always answered, "I the man, Candy. I the man!"

Then together they would sing "Who let the dogs out? Who, who, who, who let the dogs out?" Their laughter would echo down the hall. We told Roger that Candy loved him so much. Thank God Roger decided to continue being a nurse. He helped our Candy make it through the trauma of losing our precious Sonya.

The day after Sonya was buried, her parents came to see Candy in the IC critical unit. They had heard how Candy had gone rock bottom after hearing the tragic news of Sonya's death. They wanted to see Candy and wanted her to know how much they loved her and wanted her to live and get well. Mine and Bobby's hearts ached for them. "Robert and Scarlet are waiting for us in the hall," Bobby said as he ushered me from Candy's bedside to the hall where we could talk privately with Sonya's parents. Tears fell freely from all of our faces as Scarlet talked.

Scarlet told us that a few minutes before Sonya died she had asked to be lifted up to a sitting position with her pillow behind her back. She was cuddled up close, leaning her head upon mom's shoulder. Mom's wet tears fell softly against Sonya's cheek. What is so totally amazing is that right before Sonya died she asked her mother if she could go through the big gate to get to the blue sky. At first Scarlet thought Sonya was confused and talking about her close friend whose name is Sky, but then she realized her young daughter Sonya was seeing a big gold pearly gate and behind the gate's horizon was a beautiful blue sky. Sonya had just asked permission from her mother to go through that gate to get to the sky. Hot tears streaming down her cheeks, Scarlet told that she had held her sixteen-year-old daughter's swollen hand, told her how much she loved her and gave her permission to go through the gate into the blue sky. Scarlet's voice was almost a whisper as she said, "Right before Sonya died, I'll never forget how she looked at me . . . I saw a peaceful smile on her face and heard her say, I love you, Mom as she passed away."

Thus, our special friend and little angel Sonya went to be with Jesus.

Blinking back the rising tears in his eyes, Bobby told them that we believe Candy was with Sonya when Candy left us for those five minutes. Bobby and Jason had witnessed this firsthand. I had been trying to make a phone call from the waiting room and I didn't see this happen. Right before Candy died she grinned and had a look on her face that was kind of an "I know something you don't know look." Candy said, "Come play with me." Jason and Bobby both thought they heard her call Sonya's name at the end of "come play with me."

Then Candy said, "Hula Hoops . . . blue . . . trampoline . . . sky."

When we asked if Sonya owned a trampoline, her mom glowed like a sudden cozy curl of happiness just wrapped around her heart as she said, "Yes, with a blue skirt around it. I don't know how Candy could have known that." All of our eyes overflowed with tears. We knew the girls had made plans to go cruising for boys in Sonya's new red shiny sports car but we never knew anything about a trampoline. Bobby and I looked at each other and our emotions seemed to get stuck in our throats. As far as we knew, Candy didn't know anything about Sonya having a new trampoline, let alone one with a blue skirt around it. We were totally blown away with that information. We knew instantly that when our Candy had died for those five minutes she had indeed been with Sonya. It felt like we had received splashes of joy.

Wow, God never ceases to amaze us. We believe when you get to heaven, you can have whatever makes you happy. Sonya may be jumping on her trampoline with the blue skirt around it up in heaven. We believe Candy also has jumped on that trampoline with Sonya. The love and the bond those two girls shared are eternal.

Scarlet's eyes held sadness. She trembled as she continued. She told how she wouldn't allow them to take Sonya's body away until she had spend several more hours alone talking to her daughter. She combed her hair, painted her fingernails and made peace with it all before leaving Sonya's room.

Scarlet said, "For Mom, Dad and little brother Brandon the sun sank down over the mountains when our precious Sonya left us and rain came pummeling down on our roof. But Jesus wrapped us in his full embrace. We felt enveloped in his love."

Sonya's parents, Robert and Scarlet, traveled the two and a half hours drive again a few days later to see how Candy was progressing in the ICU. They held the pictures close to their heart of Sonya's recent birthday party. In the first picture, Sonya looked so pretty and beautiful as she held up her tiny matchbox red car. Scarlet told us again how Sonya had opened the small present and was told that was her new shiny red car for her 16th birthday. The next picture was the color of sunshine and happiness. Sonya stood next to her *real* car, which was new, red and real shiny. That is how we will always remember our Sonya. I would be willing to bet Sonya is driving that shiny red sports car now up in heaven. Our heart aches for Sonya's parents and for Sonya's younger brother, Brandon, who was only five. They lost something so precious, an Angel that touched the lives of so many. Our beautiful blond Sonya, with her gusto for life and faith in Jesus continues to touch lives through this book. Every single time we hear LeAnn Rimes song "You light up my life" we think of our precious Sonya. We know that she brightens up heaven with her laughter and her smile.

I felt God's closeness today. I could almost visualize some secret door in heaven that had been opened up enabling God to pour out his peace and comfort on Sonya's family. I knew that God was holding Sonya's family in his loving hands. With a rush of adrenaline, this is how Scarlet explains God's love:

Let me share a dream that God gave me. One night two weeks after Sonya had left us, I couldn't sleep. I had been awake since early morning. I felt a physical and a mental numbness as I poured out my heart to God, praying for him to carry us through this. As I drifted off into a deep peaceful sleep, I went to a faraway postcard perfect place. All around me sounds of whispering nature, birds singing, leaves rustling, a faint swish of waves and a sweet aroma of sunshine filled the air. I was shouting Sonya's name, running and hunting everywhere trying to find her. An older man came up to me and he told me to go into the cross. I looked up the hill and spotted the cross that he had pointed toward. Suddenly my legs were running up the hill. I paused for a brief second, then I actually felt myself walk directly into that huge sunlit beaming pearly white cross. Soft tears kept sliding down my cheeks and I kept screaming, "Sonya, Sonya where are you?" As I reached the top and went around a corner I saw Sonya standing in the middle of a crowd of people laughing and having fun. She looked directly at me and her eyes sparkled as her smile lit up her face. I could tell she was smack dab in the middle of happiness. I caught that smile Sonya threw my way. It was warm, inviting and melting. It felt like love, sunshine and a hug all wrapped together. As I watched, she continued laughing and having fun with the crowd who surrounded her. I believe this dream was God's way of showing me that Sonya was okay and in heaven with him. As I woke up, I could still feel the warmth of her smile that tugged at my heart. Sonya holds my heart in her hands and God holds Sonya safely in his loving arms.

And the peace of God, which transcends all understanding, will guard your hearts and your minds in Christ Jesus.
                                    —Philippians 4:7 NIV

A little bit of background:

Fast forward with me as the years go by and life goes on. This is Scarlet, Sonya's mom, fourteen years later:

I felt God nudge me today with a warm hug as I once again sat in front of Sonya's toy chest filled with all her treasured memories. Those memories are scattered all around me. Tucked away in the toy chest of my memory are the images of sunshine, laughter and butterfly kisses. All the things Sonya brought into our lives. It is hard for me to remember this as her memory flows through me and at the same time it makes me feel as though I'm enveloped in a warm hug. My favorite place to be was always inside Sonya's hugs. Long before this beautiful earth was created, God saw each moment in time, including Sonya being in heaven with him. He knew that even in heaven she would continue touching and brightening people's lives. Even fourteen years later, the world sees hope through Sonya's story.

Fourteen years later she still is influencing people through her life and her death. I have had so many people come up to me and share with me things they have done or are doing because of Sonya. This past December, I met a young woman that went to school with Sonya. She hugged me and told me she had become a social worker because of the impact that Sonya had on her when the two of them were in school together. She said that Sonya will always live in her heart. People are always saying that their lives were changed because of Sonya's testimony, her enormous faith in God, her bravery, her contagious laughter, her gusto for life; that never can get me down attitude she had and her loving spirit. Sonya wriggled right into people's hearts and what a difference she has made in their lives and in our lives.

I think often how proud our Sonya would be to know that people now call her Dad Fire Chief. Her little brother, Brandon, who was only five at the time she left us is now nineteen years old and attending a university studying Engineering. He's handsome like his Dad and he looks a lot like Sonya. He has her same gusto for life. As for me, I'm working at a school. I'm around kids all day long and that brings sunshine into my life. Sonya will always be the love of our lives. If only we could build a staircase up to heaven . . .

I asked for light, God gave me the sun, I asked for happiness and God gave me Sonya, my daughter.

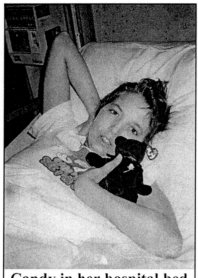

Candy in her hospital bed with some new hair

Getting out of ICU-Hooray!!!!

Pancreatitis, which was the cause of Candy's cardiac arrest way back on January 20, had kept us in the ICU until today, February 1. It felt like a flower opening up to the light as we moved back to the fifth floor into a regular hospital room with our own special nurses who had become like our family to us. We had literally lived by Candy's bedside, only leaving during the changing of the nurses' shift when they ran us out. Somehow, we seemed to have stumbled through each day in a haphazard, out of control sort of fashion. We were always on alert, expecting to have to sleep out in the waiting room but, miraculously, at the end of each three-day tour our social worker, Kay, would come by and tell us that no one else had requested our room so we had it reserved for three more days. As we moved back into the regular room, Candy still was restricted from drinking liquids. They allowed us to go home on February 10th but still she was to have no liquids, only ice. Three days later we had to go back to the clinic for a doctor visit and Candy was so disappointed when they kept the no liquid restriction on. Only ice, they once again told her. Valentine's Day came and went and we were back in the clinic on the 17th. A triumph was felt when they said, "Okay, Candy you can now have clear liquids." Three days later back in the clinic they approved her to start eating food again but watching carbohydrates. We rushed to the hospital cafeteria to eat to celebrate before going home.

Candy gets a letter

To keep her up to date on the school events and news Candy's fellow students were always sending her flyers, pictures and memos in with their handwritten get well messages. Candy's Aunt Ann would bring her a new stack to read every couple of days. The kids never forgot about Candy. They stopped by all the time, called and sent letters and cards and little love gifts.

One day as Candy was holding her pink pig pillow pal, Oink, close to her and sitting cross-legged in her bed reading all her treasured mail, she suddenly had a puzzled look come across her face and her skin looked pale as she asked, **"Mom...did I really die?"** It hit me like a brick wall and my eyes were overflowing with tears. I realized that we had never discussed it with Candy. We just sort of thought she knew. I took the letter from her shaking hands and noticed that her eyes looked glassy. Before I answered Candy, I read the letter. It was a sweet caring letter from a 6th grade boy in her school.

February 9

Dear Candy,

How are you doing? I'm fine, How about you? You may never have thought that you would ever hear from me. People say that I have changed over the summer so much. So many things have changed since you've been gone. When I first heard that you had cancer I just couldn't believe that someone so special to all of us was so very ill. I wrote 2 papers about you. Two of our best friends said I should send you the papers because what I wrote was really good. Do you remember ____'s birthday party when we were getting the apples out of the bucket with our teeth and you got the water and poured it all over me? I was soaked with water. We had the best time ever. I was wondering why did you and ____break up last year. I wish things could have been different between us. We had some good times and bad. So I will talk to you soon but the next time it will be in person. Get well, we all need you so much.

Love _____

P.S. Happy Valentine's Day

Two small pieces of paper fell from the envelope. I silently read the typed words:

January 21
A good friend has died today, but had to shock her back to life. We thank the Lord for being with her, and ask that he keep her safe, we all love Candy so much. We do not want to lose a good friend, because if we did we lose a part of ourselves. Candy is like family to us. She is like a sister to all of us. Candy is smart, beautiful, and very brave. So we all hope that she will make it through this because we need her so very much.

January 27
The Lord has heard our prayers and Candy is doing well. Candy has done a lot for people, but the number 1 thing that she has done for us has been being our friend. It seems when Candy got sick we all came together and supported her all the way. If we can do this why can't we all come together more? We are all so glad that Candy is doing well and hope that the Lord will stay by her side. We all love Candy so much, we do not want to lose a good friend. Candy is so special to all of us. We would not want to think what we would do if we lose someone very special to us. Candy will always be a good friend to all of us, because she will live in our hearts forever.

Wow! The letter touched my heart and soul way down deep but all this at once was overwhelming for little twelve-year-old fragile Candy. Suddenly she was afraid and asked questions like:

-How do I know it won't happen again when something else bottoms out or goes wrong?

-Where was I at when I died?

-Where did I go?

-How did they bring me back?

-Why did it happen, Mom? Why me?

Question after question filled the air. I paused and took a deep breath before answering. This is how I explained it to her. "Candy, the best way I can describe this to you is that Jesus kicked butt." She looked at me now smiling, "He kicked butt?"

"Yes, Jesus kicked butt. He got tired of what that old devil was doing to you. That old devil he wanted you so bad. He tried everything to get you because he doesn't want you to be around to do what God has in store for you to do. But, Candy, we wouldn't let him have you. We made God keep his promise of healing you. We held him to his word, his promise. So you see, Jesus did kick butt and put that old devil on his way. He told that devil that you belong to him and that he could no longer keep you down. It's over. It's finished. It's all settled, is what Jesus told that old devil. You want to know how I know this?"

Candy's shoulders straightened up and her eyes began twinkling. "Yes, Mom how do you know this?"

I went on to explain it this way: "While you were really sick in the IC unit mine, your Dad's and Jason's nerves were shot and we couldn't sleep because we wanted to be by your side all the time. We were afraid if we left you for a minute something might happen. Our complete focus was on keeping you alive. Nothing else mattered. One time, I don't remember if it was day or night, I had gone into the little rented room down the hall from the ICU. The room had only a TV, fold-out sofa, bathtub and no toilet. It might have been one of the times Cat, my best friend, had sat with you in ICU while I rested. From total exhaustion, I collapsed on the fold-out bed. God revealed to me in a dream that what had happened had to happen, and it had to happen that exact way. You had to die. He told me that there was no other way his will could be accomplished. You had to go farther than rock bottom before he could take complete control. So in my mind, I visualized Jesus kicking the devil's butt. When I awoke something told me to pick up the hospital Bible on the little table. It immediately opened to Luke 8. I just couldn't wait to tell your daddy what Jesus had revealed to me. Aunt Raylene and Uncle Eugene came by that same day to the hospital and I couldn't wait to share my newly discovered revelation with them. It had been so clear and peaceful. God always finds a way to hug us."

Candy then reached for her Bible and together we read Luke 8 starting at verse 42. It wasn't hard to find because I had it circled in red and highlighted in yellow as Candy's story. I went on to explain that what God heals doesn't come unhealed. "You are not going to die again, at least not anytime soon. There is something so special that God has in store for you, Candy, that he wouldn't allow that old devil to have you. Believe me that old devil wanted you so bad. Who knows, you may be the one who discovers a cure for cancer or invents something spectacular or maybe it will be your children who do that. It might even be someone who God puts directly in your path for you to make a difference to and that person may end up doing something spectacular. It might be something that you and your husband do together for God. Who knows? I have no doubt because you have touched so many lives. Candy, God kept you alive for some special reason. He has something special that he needs you to accomplish."

For we wrestle not against flesh and blood, but

against principalities, against powers, against the
rulers of the darkness of this world, against
spiritual wickedness in high places.
  Above all, taking the shield of faith, wherewith
ye shall be able to quench all the fiery darts of the
wicked...Praying always.
                            —Ephesians 6:12, 16, 18 (KJV)

I enthusiastically asked Candy if she remembered anything about being in heaven. I told her that right before she had died she grinned and had a look on her face that was kind of an "I know something you don't know look." And that her dad and brother had thought she said. "Come play with me, Sonya . . . Hula Hoops . . . blue . . . trampoline . . . sky." I went on to explain to Candy that we believe she was with Sonya when she died for those five minutes. We believe she and Sonya were jumping together on her trampoline with the blue skirt around it. I asked Candy if she remembered anything about Sonya having that trampoline and she said she didn't know Sonya had one.

It's our hope that someday Jesus will allow Candy to remember bits and pieces of what heaven was like but for now he has erased that from her memory. We can only imagine how awesome heaven was to our twelve year old Candy Kisses; what it felt like, looked like, sounded like, smelled like and even tasted like. We wonder who she met there. We wonder if the ones who love her in heaven were there to greet her. We wonder if she was able to sit on Jesus' lap. There have been times while she and I have been out shopping that Candy would get a delightful smile on her face and brief whiff of a scent in the air and I have heard her say, "That smells like heaven." I've asked her why that smells like heaven and she would reply, "I don't know for sure, but it just smells like heaven." I would try my best to pick up that same brief whiff of a scent but I couldn't sense it, only she could.

If God be for us, who can be against us?
—Romans 8:31 KJV

An Interview with Candy

Candy and her cousin Wendy were always real close. I remember when Candy was little she didn't want to be left alone, so each Sunday during church services we could hear Candy screaming through the air vents. I thought we would never get Candy to enjoy church. For our little toddler the only way we finally discovered Candy would go into a church Sunday School room was for her to sit next to her cousin Wendy. That was Candy's comfort zone. The two of them were big pals. Wendy took it really hard when Candy was in the ICU, so very sick. I'll never forget the look of horror on Wendy's face when she stepped inside the ICU for the first time to see her cousin Candy on a breathing respirator battling for her life. Heartache and pain were written all over Wendy's face.

Wendy was so excited to see Candy getting well and back in school. Many people had doubts whether Candy would live to see her thirteen birthday but here she was soon reaching that milestone. Wendy was on the staff for their school's newsletter called "7th 8th Inquiring Minds Class of 2002-2003." Her position was called "Interview & Things To Do" so she interviewed Candy. Here's that interview:

CANDY

As many of you know, my cousin Candy Sparks has leukemia. Since she is currently in the seventh grade I thought it would be a good idea to do a short interview.

WH: If you could choose one word that describes your life what would it be and why?

CS: *"Miracles. Because without the miracles of God, I wouldn't be here now."*

WH: Now that you've come this far where do you want your life to go from here?

CS: *"I want to become a hematologist known as 'Dr. Sparks, Medicine Woman'."*

WH: If you had a one-way plane ticket to anywhere in the world where would you go?

CS: *'Hawaii."*

WH: Who is the person you look up to the most?

CS: *"My Big Bubba, Jason Sparks"*

WH: What are you looking forward to the most as a teen?

CS: *"Hanging out with friends."*

WH: Do you have any last words that you would like to add?

CS: *"I just want to tell everyone to be thankful and appreciate everything, and live life to the fullest. I would also like to thank everyone for all their support and just being there for me."*

Candy's birthday is at the end of May. She will be 13 years old. She's come a long way since her last birthday which she spent in the hospital. Now Candy enjoys riding her bicycle and 4-wheeler. She's coming along fast, but she still needs your support and prayers.

God Hiding

I chuckle each time I hear someone say, "Where was God during all of this?" Or how about, "I hope they find God before it is too late." Just the thought of that makes me laugh out loud.

In my mind I picture a person literally going out

searching for God, as if God were lost. Can't you just imagine looking high and low, behind huge trees, down slippery hill slopes or even on top of the highest mountains and hearing them saying, "Where is God? I know he is here somewhere? If I keep searching I'm bound to find him." Well, my friend, God doesn't hide. You don't have to go out searching for him. He isn't lost. In fact God hasn't moved at all, never has and never will. We're the ones who have moved. The wonderful news is God will come to you, just like he came to my family. He will never leave nor forsake you. We have his promise on that. God comes to find us in the midst of our sorrows. He never leaves us where he finds us, unless we insist. Every time we think of God it is because he first had us on his mind. I believe that the Lord is always the initiator. Twenty four hours a day God is there, backing us up, coaching and guiding us forward. He's always ready to listen.

"Jesus, you lead; I want to follow." Amen

Pennies from Heaven

June 1998

I started back to work today. It was good to get back to BellSouth where I had worked since I was barely 16. I'd been on leave of absence since Candy was diagnosed with leukemia on that terrible April Fool's Day back in 1997. I worked only a few days in November, December and January. Remember, January had been when Candy had gone rock bottom. For weeks before time for me to return to work my left shoulder began hurting really badly. My chiropractor, Dr. Gay, had said my bursitis sack in my left shoulder had received intensive damage. Since I had returned to work, the pain seemed constant. I couldn't raise my arm up or down and it ached and ached.

Candy would cry when she heard me say what had caused the damage. While she was so sick and couldn't walk she had to put all her weight on my left arm. I had to literally lift her in and out of the bathtub as well as brace her against my arm when as she walked. On advice from my wise husband, I had tried an old timey remedy cure. Underneath a wide bandage I had placed two copper pennies against my shoulder. The copper seemed to pull some of the pain out. Unable to find a copper bracelet for sale, I continued performing this same ritual with the pennies taped to my shoulder for weeks until suddenly the pain vanished.

I was reminded of the copper pennies today as I read an article. It was about a grandma who always proclaimed that every time you find a penny you should think about the inscription written on that penny, *IN GOD WE TRUST*. It's a special reminder from God to trust him.

Now I have a new perception about those shiny coppery coins you find everywhere. I had always heard you should only pick up a penny with heads up because bottoms up pennies would bring bad luck. Now, whenever I spot a penny on the ground, I'll pick it up and imagine it's God wrapping his arms around me in a warm hug and whispering. "I haven't forgotten you. Just keep trusting me." Maybe that trust was what healed my shoulder rather than the copper in the pennies.

Afraid God would sap me

Candy began to grow stronger and slowly, very slowly, her little body began to heal.

As I returned to work, I was no longer a workaholic like I was before she got sick. I loved my job and how I had missed the fast pace of corporate America. Returning to work, I was afraid that if I didn't do everything perfectly, if I slipped for just a moment, I feared that for some reason God would sap me and things would again take a plunge downward. One day my car was in the shop so I drove Bobby's pickup truck to work. It was a big truck and as I backed out of the parking space, I accidently hit a tall lamp pole causing it to dent and bend forward. That old devil tried to convince me to leave and pretend that it never happened. It's like I could hear him whispering in my ear. I started to leave but just couldn't so with my face almost in my hands, shoulders drooping, I walked back inside and asked to see the Security Manager. I told her of my dilemma and expected to have to pay big bucks, which I didn't have for my mistake of hitting and bending the lamp pole over. She hugged me and said, "Honey, that's okay. It happens all the time. Don't worry about it." I realized then that God doesn't sap you. Later that night this verse jumped out at me from my Bible.

He that handleth a matter wisely shall find good: and whoso trusteth in the Lord, happy is he.
—Proverbs 16:20

Warm Healing Hands

While I was getting ready for work today, Candy woke up hurting real badly in her lower stomach and back. Her daddy heard her crying through the monitor by her bed. He's such a good daddy. He cuddled up on the bed next to his little girl and put his warm hand on her little belly. We have always told him he has warm healing hands.Later that night, Candy told us that after her daddy and I left for work, she asked Jesus to help her belly stop hurting. She went back to sleep and when she woke up it wasn't hurting anymore. When she tested her blood sugar that morning she couldn't seem to get her little finger to bleed so in faith she silently proclaimed, "If I trust in

Jesus, the blood will come." She went on to explain, "Magically a perfect drop fell on the test strip." What faith to be so young!

God in your back pocket

A girl told me the other day that she was going to sell her house in two months.

To myself, I wondered, *"How can you be so sure?"*

She proclaimed, "I told God that's what I need to do and I asked him to sell my house for me. It's going to sell in two months. I know that."

My God is not a God I carry around in my pocket. However, my God does have my back covered. I don't think of him in my pocket, rather I see him holding my hand. I feel his warm hugs in the beauty of his creation. I hear his whisper of guidance. I feel his strength. If I start to fall, he lifts me up. I feel his love as if a warm blanket enveloped around me. He makes me feel like I'm the most important person in the whole wide world to him. I'm nothing. I shouldn't even be allowed to say his name. If Jesus could be used up, I'd keep him all to myself. I have found that the more I share him, the more there is of him.

This was taped to my computer at BellSouth for many years and now is taped to my computer in my den at home.

Sparks' motto:
The more love I give..............the more love I have available to give.

The more I help others...........suddenly I'm able to help others even more.

I'm so glad JESUS can never be used up!

Believe you deserve to be happy. Say "I open my arms wide to the very best God has for me today."

Our Journey

JOHN 11:25

July
through
December

I'm holding you, Jesus, to your promises

July

Remembering Independence Day last year, we were living in the hospital and sleeping by Candy's bed, but Dr. Berkow had allowed us to escape on the July 4th to go home for just a few days. Friends and relatives wanted to bring us some barbeque but it wouldn't have tasted very good with hot salty tears dripping from our faces. This 4th of July a year later, however, we were excited to be home. Candy had looked so forward to helping her daddy grill out but she began throwing up and her lower back cramped. All day long on the 4th her little back continued to cramp and she couldn't keep any food down. It brought back painful memories of last summer when she was so very sick.

My eyes brimming with tears, I shut the bathroom door and dropped to my knees in prayer. I told Jesus that I knew with all my heart that the Bible was true and pure and that I could hold on to its message. I wasn't trying to tell God what to do. He had already told me what he would do. I just reminded him that I'm holding him to it.

...I am the Lord that healeth thee [healeth Candy].
—Exodus 15:26

As I prayed, I remembered that I had always reiterated to Candy that the Bible is God's Word. I wanted her to believe that when the angels in heaven hear God's written word spoken they will if necessary, all come down to earth to make sure his word is carried out. It's going to happen! I wanted her to know that if God shows you his word written down in the

Bible all you have to do is believe. Believe with all your heart even though what you are seeing with your eyes happens to be completely different. *I had tried to teach Candy that the reason faith is so very wonderful is that you don't have to figure out how to make it happen. All you have to do is believe.*

Suddenly, I felt a strong sense of peace as I remembered my special verse that God had shown me:

...Fear not: believe only, and she [Candy] shall be made whole [well].

—Luke 8:50

I thanked God and went to bed, knowing that he is in total control. Her daddy and I both slept all night long that night with Candy. She was afraid everything was happening all over again. How scary to be barely thirteen, knowing that you had literally died for five minutes and afraid it might happen again. The way I explained to Candy what had happened the night she died was that Jesus had kicked butt. That night Jesus had battled that old devil for Candy and of course Jesus won and sent that old devil on his way, proclaiming that Candy belonged to him. That always made Candy smile and her cute little dimple light up. She liked the kicked butt theory.

It's no wonder Candy finds comfort having her daddy's warm hand against her little cramping sides and back. Her daddy's hands are warm and healing, so all night Candy wanted daddy's healing hands placed on her back or side to help ease the pain. She reminded us of the stories that we often had told her. Both Candy and big Bubba Jason had always gotten a thrill out of hearing that while I was pregnant with each of them in my belly their little bodies would follow the heat of their daddy's warm hand. Bobby would move his hand and they would wiggle until they were again right under the heat of his hand. If they knotted up in a ball that hurt, Bobby's warm hand made them relax and he could literally move them by simply moving his hand. You could watch my fat pregnant belly and see their little bodies wiggle until they nestled under the heat of his hand. Jason did that when I was pregnant with him and then when I was pregnant with Candy she did the same thing. After each was born and had stomach aches their pain was eased by laying them against their daddy's warm chest. So it's no wonder Candy feels healing with her daddy's warm hand upon her cramping little back.

As Candy cried from hurting and from being afraid, I shared my faith with her. I repeated my special bible verse that Jesus had given me.

...Fear not: believe only, and she [Candy] shall be made whole [well].
—Luke 8:50

I explained that was Jesus telling us that she would be okay. Exhausted, Candy finally went to sleep.

The next day I called into work to tell them I needed a vacation day. Jason and I left early, taking Candy to the clinic. Her liver and kidney functions were high and she had a trace of blood in her urine. I said a silent, "Thank you, Dear Jesus" as Dr. Berkow told us that all her counts and organ functions looked good and that she was going to be fine. He did however, tell us to hold up on her methotrexate shot and he told us not to give her the chemo 6MP pills at night for a week. I had hoped Dr. Berkow wouldn't mention to Candy that she was due for a spinal tap again next week but he did. Her little back already hurting from all those previous spinal taps and knowing that she would have another one next week must have been very frightening for a little girl. It's hard to see the rainbows when you are still battling the storms but Candy, my little hero, did see rainbows.

Faith is daring the soul to go beyond what the eyes can see.

Three strikes and you're out

November

Candy had another spinal tap and chemo in her spine today. Satan keeps trying to put doubt in my mind about the results of those tests. Satan and his angels are very real and powerful here on earth. In the months past he had many field days destroying our family. Constant hurt and pain he put in our minds and in our hearts daily. Satan hates knowing that my faith and love for Jesus are now rooted down deep. He can't stand the fact that I want to shout my praises for Jesus from the highest mountaintops.

Candy cried as she stepped from the scales and realized she had lost another pound. Later in the treatment room, Nurse Meredith reached for the long spinal tap needle but it dropped to the floor. She sent a nurse to retrieve a replacement but soon found out that the clinic was completely out of that type of needle. She was given a replacement needle in a different size. While doing the spinal tap, the rain drops, as we call them, dripped into the vials. Meredith made the comment, "If Candy had gained one more pound this needle wouldn't have worked." Meaning the whole painful process would then have needed to be redone. Tears streamed down Candy's cheeks. She was always awake during this painful procedure. She said, "That's why God made me lose a pound!"

(Meredith had not known Candy had lost another pound and had been upset over losing weight.)

Faith as small as a mustard seed can move a mountain.

At home later that afternoon before clinic closing time I called the clinic for the results. Candi, one of the clinic nurses, said the protein and glucose results were normal but the results were not in to show if leukemia cells were present. We were praying hard that the leukemia cells were not back.

Doubt #1 came in loud and clear from the devil!
This had never happened before. The results always come in together. What could the holdup be? Satan reminded me that Candy's doctor, Dr. Berkow, was out of town.

Doubt #2 came in loud and clear from the devil!
Earth to Candy's Mom. *The nurse has the results. You know she does. It's a cover-up. She wants to wait and let Dr. Berkow tell you. Satan whispered to me: You know that's the truth. You heard it in her voice. Remember, .you asked if the results would be in tomorrow. Her reply was, "Should be." Who is she fooling? Not you . . . You heard it in the nurse's tone . . . The results are bad. The nurse has been trained to let the doctor be the one to tell the heartbreaking news . . . The leukemia has come back and you know it.*
It's like l felt the flicker of an angel's wing rub against my shoulder.
No! No! Listen: **Heaven to Candy's Mom, the angel said**.....*Jesus doesn't operate like this. He doesn't get pleasure out of your heartache and pain. He's very faithful. You can trust him . . . Remember:* **Fear not: believe only and Candy shall be made whole (well).**

I decided to take my Bible, go into my bathroom, shut the door, get on my knees and ask Jesus what's going on. It was November so dark comes early and the room was completely dark. The exact second I touched the light switch to turn the light on, what happens but the bulb blows. It scared me and I took a step backward as I pulled my hand away from the light switch and I thought, Wow! What timing that old devil has. He just caused the light bulb to blow.

Doubt #3 came in loud and clear from the devil!

I could almost hear Satan laughing as he whispered to me: Bulb blowing out, this has to be a bad omen, foretelling you that Jesus doesn't want you to confront him. The leukemia has come back and you know it. Just face the facts.

Suddenly, I remembered that the Holy Spirit has given me a tremendous gift of faith. In January, my faith was so strong that I was able to look beyond death to know, without a shadow of a doubt, that Jesus is faithful to his word. I don't need a light on to pray. It doesn't matter that the room is scary dark. Jesus is my light. If necessary I'll talk with Jesus in the dark.

Just then Jesus' warm response floated from my mind into my heart:

Jesus' message came in loud and clear!!!

Mary, there were 3 vials of spinal fluid. Different people tested each vial. It's okay that the results are coming in at different times. Remember, **Fear not, believe only . . .**

In my mind, I finished the sentence, and **Candy shall be made whole (well).** When I glanced up and opened the door so I could see again, I noticed that same verse written on a small piece of paper taped to the bathroom mirror where I had placed it months before. I knew then, without a doubt, that the results would be perfect. I even waited an extra day before calling back to the clinic. When I did talk with Meredith her cheerful voice assured me, "Candy spinal results were beautiful. See you soon." (Praise God!!!)

You will not stumble while on your knees.

Ten Words I promise will change your life.

Do you want to know a formula that will guarantee your happiness and peace, no matter what situation you are in? Ten words that will fill your emptiness, fears and troubles, replacing them with love that envelops your whole being? Ten words that you can hold onto with total assurance that peace, joy and divine guidance are yours. I promise you this will work. Get several index cards or small pieces of paper and write this:

God is Good! God is Merciful! God is in Control!

Put those cards where you can see them often. I taped one by my bathroom mirror, another on my car dash, another one stored in my change purse and one above my kitchen stove. Ten words will sink deep into your mind. They are powerful words. If you wake up during the night say, ***God is Good! God is Merciful! God is in Control!*** Then turn over and go back to sleep. Say the words to yourself while you are in the elevator or grocery shopping or anywhere you might be, day or night. I even have mine attached to my computer. Before too long those ten words will flow automatically from your heart into your life; things will begin going better for you. You will have strength, joy and peace that you never knew existed before. You will know God's love and know that he is in control. Nothing is too big or difficult for God. He can do everything. God has no limitations or boundaries. His resources and power go on forever.

When my Candy Kisses was sick I needed something I could hold in my hand that I felt was powerful and strong while I myself felt weak and very afraid. My strength came from ten words written on a small index card that I held in my hand and then in my heart. Before I knew it I began to believe that God was good, merciful and in control. Yes, in control of this terrible ordeal my family was battling. That old devil got us down. He kicked us and stomped us. The devil loves doing that. Hold onto these ten words and God will pull you up and bless you more than you could ever imagine. Continue to keep these ten words flowing from your heart to your mind. Keep saying them the rest of your life. Before too long, those ten words will be as much a part of you and as natural as breathing. Want to make these ten little words even more powerful? If you do, add a few more words to the end of these ten powerful words. Add: I love you, Jesus.

He shall call upon me, and I will answer him: I will be with him in trouble;
I will deliver him, and honour him.
—Psalm 91:15 KJV

Christmas Eve, a voice says walk now

My office closed early and when I got home Candy was sitting on brother's bed grinning ear to ear with joy sparking in her eyes. With her big dimple shining she said, "I have a present for you." She lifted herself off her big brother's bed and proceeded to walk unattended out of his doorway, down the long hallway, through the kitchen, dining room area, stopping by the back door. I was elated with happiness and planted a kiss on her forehead as I held her close to me. As I tried to blink back a tear I asked, "When did you first do that? I didn't know you could walk again."

This is how she described what had happened: "Mom, this morning when I woke up I felt nervous. It was like a voice or something was telling me that I needed to get up and walk. I heard it loud and clear. I thought to myself, *you know I can't walk* but somehow I knew if I didn't get up right then and walk that I'd never walk again. I wasn't really afraid, just real excited so I got up. I was surprised when I actually was able to walk slowly all the way from my room into Jason's room. I stood by his bed and shook him awake. It sort of scared Bubba. He woke up and looked at me and he said, "How did you get in here?" I told him I had walked all by myself and he immediately said, "But you can't walk." I said, "But Bubba, I did walk." When I told him how it all happened, he was happy and had me walking all through the house. We practiced all day. I wanted to keep this a secret so I could surprise you and Daddy on Christmas morning but you know little ol' me, I just can't keep a secret.

Strangely, an image popped into my mind and I had a sudden flashback . . .

I saw again the doctors around Candy's hospital bed in the one-day surgery and I heard them telling us Candy probably would never walk again. She had no feeling in her feet and her toes just wouldn't move. While she was so sick in bed for so long, there was serious damage done to the muscles in her feet and legs. At one point we were told that unless Candy responded to some intensive physical therapy really fast, her fragile bones might begin to break as we tried to move her.

All at once, my mind spinning in another direction remembered a more recent image. I visualized Candy just a few days ago crying as she took a bath. What was it Candy had spoken to me? "It's not fair that I can't walk. The other kids walk." I remember drying her tears and saying, "Candy, let's remember God's verse he told you? *I can do all things through Christ which strengtheneth me.* All things, Candy, that includes walking. Hold God to that!"

All at once Candy's big smile brought me back from my flashbacks to reality. A new rush of meaning and understanding flowed through me. It had taken almost nine months but thank God she had just walked. I thought to myself, **Candy Kisses, My Miracle from God**. Later that day when Daddy came home Candy showed him how she could walk all by herself. "Big Daddy," as she calls him, had tears of joy streaming down his face.

12/9/98

The best Christmas present I have ever given is the Christmas present I gave last year to my family. It was special because I was alive after having A.L.L. My mom told me that was the greatest gift ever. Because I was alive and well and with my family. The gift was me being alive.

The best Christmas gift ever

The Dream (aka: nightmare)

December 1998

I'm standing in our pasture on top of the big grassy hill, the day bright and beautiful and the sun warm against my skin. I embrace my surroundings with awe and wonder. I love this place. It's where we had planned to build our new house. The grass is so green, the sky baby blue and everything so peaceful and tranquil. I feel like I can see forever. This place is postcard perfect. At the bottom of the hill, I see my Candy standing close to the pond. Her little hand goes up to wave at me. How I love her!

From behind me, I hear wings flapping. I turn to see a big huge bird flying low. Its wings expanded appear to be about 10 or 12 feet in diameter. It's beautiful but seems to have some fierceness about it. It's almost hawk-like. I duck as it goes over my head. It's flying straight toward Candy. Oh, no! I run with all my might, screaming at the top of my lungs, "No! No! No!" I know if that huge bird were to take my Candy away, I'll never find her again. She'll be so afraid. Where will it take her? How will I ever find her?

All at once, that big wild hawk-like bird reaches Candy and sweeps her up. I once saw a chicken hawk sweep low and pick up one of our baby chicks the same way, taking it away, never to be seen again. I see Candy's little legs kicking back and forth as she tries to free herself. The bird holds on to her tightly. I see the panic in Candy's eyes. I can't get there fast enough but I'm running so fast. The huge hawk-like bird is flying over the pond with Candy in its claws. I scream, "Oh no, no!" It's holding Candy under the water as it flies over the pond. It's trying to drown her, trying to keep her head underwater. I'm treading through the water, my arms outstretched. I feel stuck in the mud and my screams seem soundless. I'm trying desperately to reach my Candy.

I'm almost to her. "Please, Jesus!" I hear myself shout...

Then, I feel a gentle shake and hear my name being called. As my husband wakes me, he breaks the dream into a thousand pieces.

In my distress I cried unto the Lord, and he heard me.

—Psalm 120:1 KJV

Our Victory and Triumphs

We began having little triumphs in our lives. They felt so good. How we rejoiced over each victory. It felt like another thin layer of pain and helplessness had been slowly stripped away with each added victory. I remember how we jumped up and down elated in happiness when the heart doctor's test revealed the hole in Candy's heart was no longer there. It would no longer be pumping that deadly candidiasis fungal infection throughout her little body. I remember again jumping up and down with total delight when the final CT scan revealed the deadly infection was gone that had been in all Candy's vital organs, including her liver, kidneys, spleen, brain and even behind her eyes. I remember how wonderful it felt each time urgent prayers were answered for Candy's blood count to show enough of her own platelets being made. I remember when the whole community had joined us to pray when what we needed was for Candy's red blood count to reach a certain level. I remember one time Candy's cousin, Leon, was so elated with happiness that his wife said he actually went outside and shouted out loud.

All the many times Candy had to be put asleep to have her esophagus dilated, then one bright blessing-filled day, we learned no more dilatations were needed. We had won the victory and her feeding tube in her stomach and that ugly string that went down the side of her mouth, into her esophagus and out her lower stomach was removed. We thank God for that feeding tube and for that string that was used to dilate her esophagus but now she felt and looked so much better without both. No one could ever imagine how very much Candy now enjoys eating. She never throws food away. We laugh at her because while she is eating one meal she is busy planning what her next meal will be, the whole time her dimple shining.

I remember when our prayers were answered and Candy's little toes began to move again.

Each little baby step made toward Candy being able to walk again and all that painful therapy finally paying off. Being told Candy may not ever be able to walk again, no way that was for us.

Now she walks and runs. Early in Candy's sickness, she found this Bible verse and we then knew how things would turn out.

But they that wait upon the Lord shall renew their strength; they shall mount up with wings as eagles; they shall run, and not be weary; and they shall walk, and not faint. Isaiah 40:31

Candy loved that verse and she found it herself. I remember her saying, "Mom, it says, shall walk so that is what we claimed, shall walk. I remembered how Candy wouldn't allow us to park in a handicap space when she was in the wheelchair. She would say, "Mom, leave that handicap space for some old woman or old man that needs it." I thought she needed that handicap parking space more than they did, but Candy always insisted on leaving it for someone else. I remembered once inside the stores she would have me help her sit in a grocery buggy. Her little bald head uncovered and her little dimple shining, she was more concerned with helping others than in helping herself. Now she is finally able to walk again. Hooray!!

The last spinal tap needed brought joy unspeakable to us. What about no more chemo needed? We're cancer free. Hooray!! Imagine our triumphs and joy unspeakable when finally they removed Candy's central line underneath her arm. No more wires and plugs attached to her.

Early on, Magic Moments had granted Candy her wish of a hot tub. They gave her a beautiful Jacuzzi Whirlpool bath complete with jets, blue interior that lights up and looks like an ocean and a built-in molded seat for Candy. The hot tub would seat eight but it would be at least two and a half years out before the hot tub could be used so we had it stored with a plastic covering over it just awaiting Candy's heroic time of actually being able to use the hot tub. A good friend, David, out of love, built Candy a big porch that would hold her hot tub. He built it by himself and made it extra sturdy to hold the heavy weight of the tub. Now Candy and her friends could listen to music and relax in her very own hot tub. Hooray!!

Can you imagine Candy's joy at being able to lie down in the bathtub again and take a bubble bath and be able to get her whole little body wet? No wonder she now loves to take bubble baths and soak. Without her wires attached, she could get in the tub by herself and soak for hours. No more pulling that big burdensome pole around that connected her pumps to her. No more carrying around that little black bag of intravenous liquid food that was connected to her, feeding her 24/7. No more being hooked up at Children's Hospital to get blood or chemo. No more

Mom, Dad and brother Jason living at the hospital with her. Home felt so good.

Candy survived not one but these three life threatening illnesses:
1) Acute Lymphocytic Leukemia (ALL)
2) The very serious Disseminated Candidiasis. Most people who get this live only a week.
3) Pancreatitis, which also caused cardiac arrest for five minutes. Her heart had to be shocked back to beating again.

Candy began going back to school. She made Homecoming Court and was part of the Color Guard. During her senior year she was president of the student body SGA (Student Government Association). It was a cute site, little Candy, barely over five feet tall, being the right arm of their loved principal, whom we fondly called Coach Kellogg. Candy graduated with an advanced high school diploma and a 4.0 average. She became very active with the youth at Calvary Baptist Church. I remember one day the church was filled to the rim as Candy stood at the podium and gave her testimony. One man sitting next to me said, "When Jesus comes again, I want to be sitting next to Candy so he will take me when he takes her." Not a dry eye was in the congregation. Since then she has given her testimony at several big youth rallies. Candy talks to God like he is standing right beside her, her best friend. She soon became a Vacation Bible School Teacher and Director then a regular Sunday school teacher. She worked part time at Calvary Community Daycare. After graduation she worked fulltime at the Daycare teaching three and four year olds while she attended college.

I would like to reiterate what Candy always said and still says:

"My dream is that someday they will find a cure for cancer, so people won't have to go through what I had to endure. You don't appreciate what you have until suddenly you don't have it or it is taken from you. People just aren't thankful enough. I believe you should say a prayer of thanks every time you are able to drink a sip of water, walk or even when you are able to lie down in the bathtub to soak. Those things and many other things were taken from me for a long time. Things we take for granted are all gifts and blessings from God and can be taken away from us in a blink of the eye."

As her Mom, I still say, "If you want to see how good God is look at my Candy Kisses."

With all this being said, the greatest triumph of all came when Jesus took Candy's hand and brought her back to life after being in heaven with him and young Sonya for about five minutes.

We pray that God will bless you much and that this book will help you in whatever chapter you are now going through in your own life. Just keep holding onto Jesus' hand.

For with God nothing shall be impossible.
—Luke 1:37

And blessed is she that believed: for there shall be a performance of those things which were told her from the Lord.
—Luke 1:45

For he that is mighty hath done to me great things; and holy is his name.

And his mercy is on them that fear him from generation to generation.
—Luke 1:49-50

To give light to them that sit in darkness and in the shadow of death, to guide our feet into the way of peace.
—Luke 1:79

What about this "ah-ha" moment.

The other day, coming home after a drizzling rain, I noticed a color blast in front of my car. The light blue sky became an artist's canvas. I watched in awe as a brilliant dynamic rainbow appeared from nowhere. I'm oohing and aahing at the wonder of it all when a second rainbow materializes. **Another candy kiss from God**.

I have seen two other double rainbows since Candy got sick. One in the sky over the Relay for Life Cancer Survivor luncheon and one greeted us over the breathtaking mountains just as we got out of our car in Gatlinburg at our family reunion.

A grandma's dream

One thing about us grandmas, or Mims as I am called, we love sharing grandchildren stories. What a blessing from God they are. Today I met a lady who couldn't stop talking about how much she loves her four-year-old granddaughter, the light of her life.

Every grandma has a story. Here's hers:

Almost in a whisper she said, "My seven-year-old grandson was killed in a car accident a few years back. I never blamed God, but I was very angry at him."

With a heavy heart, I answered her, "It's okay to be angry with God."

As tears filled her eyes, she said, "I questioned God, *WHY! WHY GOD DID YOU TAKE MY GRANDSON?* He was only seven years old, so young and such a good boy." She seemed to drift into a different time as her eyes filled with tears and she continued. "Then one night as I slept I had a dream. I saw God." The woman's voice grew stronger as she said, "God even hugged me and he explained why my grandson had to die. I felt love and peace. At that moment, I understood the exact why. He revealed it to me. I understood perfectly. My anger at God was dissipated, gone." She seemed to be in deep thought as she continued, "It's strange, but I remember I even thanked God for taking my grandson. What God had told me was totally awesome and believable. When I awoke, the dream was still very much on my mind and to this day I remember that dream very vividly."

As I listened to her story, I couldn't wait to hear the reason why her grandson had to die. Her eyes were no longer liquid with tears but seemed to be twinkling with joy. Just then I felt a warm teardrop slide down my own cheek as I listened. "The only thing is . . ." She took a deep breath. "I can't tell you why my grandson had to die. I know in my dream God told me why, and at that time I understood perfectly, but when I awoke that memory had been erased from my mind. I remember the warmth of God, and the overwhelming sense of feeling so loved and so happy. I felt total peace. That peace is what helped me through my grief."

As I looked at her in amazement, I knew that it didn't even bother her that God had erased "the why" from her memory. Before she left, the woman said to me, "God gave me a little granddaughter, lives next door to me, the light of my life. My heart overflows with love every time she puts her little arms around my neck and whispers, I love you, Granny. God's timing in giving her to me was perfect. If she had been born too soon after my grandson's death I wouldn't have been allowed to grieve. A couple of years passed and God gave me my granddaughter. God knew I needed a small bundle of joy to funnel all my love to, my own special angel. Oh, she doesn't replace my grandson, because nothing ever could, but she fills that void in my life with an unbelievable joy. I thank God for telling me why my grandson died even though I can't remember what he told me. I know that God gave me exactly what I needed and now he has truly blessed me with a special angel, my granddaughter."

I looked at her and thought, *"Wow, how happy she truly is, she glows from the inside out."*

As she walked away, she turned back and said, "God is so awesome!" I had to agree. GOD is so awesome!

Log of our long journey

This is a log recorded by Wonder Woman, as Candy calls her. Everyone should be as lucky as Candy and Jason are to have an Aunt Ann like this. At a very young age, Aunt Ann (Mary Ann Hardy) was diagnosed with polio. Since then she has survived three different kinds of cancer: uterus, colon and recently breast cancer. Aunt Ann's husband also is a survivor of prostate cancer. Candy's mom and dad were in no shape to keep a log while Candy was sick but her Aunt Ann documented this for us, in her own words. Aunt Ann even had her first granddaughter born just a few months after Candy was diagnosed with leukemia. (Candy felt like God gave her a precious little baby cousin named Nikki to love and hold. Candy still calls her, Mini Me.) Even with her plate already full, Aunt Ann was always there for us. After what she and Candy had endured with cancer, it was Aunt Ann's dream to form her own cancer support group. Thus was created, ***"Friends Helping Friends, Cancer Survivors and Supporters."***

Aunt Ann's dream is now a reality with quarterly very upbeat meetings or should I say parties that include supper, guest speakers, singers, gifts and door prizes. She is making a difference is many people's lives by the creation of this support group. Thank God for Aunt Ann. This log shows the ups and downs of our journey. You can see why Candy's mom says Candy is her hero. You can see what all Candy had to endure and how she weathered the storm all the time having that cute little dimple of hers shining. Candy has touched so many lives. Whatever storms you are battling in your life, just remember by holding on to Jesus' hand you can also have hope. At the end of the storm the rainbows are breathtaking.

April 1997

1st Dr. Bearman took blood test and suspected leukemia. He sent us directly to Children's Hospital.

2nd Very painful bone marrow tests confirmed ALL (Acute Lymphocytic Leukemia) and chemo was started.

3rd Two pints of blood given. (Candy has A positive blood). Candy had a very painful spinal with chemo. Also steroids began. Dr. Berkow talked with us, then explained situation to Candy. She was upset because she would miss school which she loved.

4th More chemo.

5th Found heart problem.

6th More chemo then we got to go home.

7th Candy was able to stay up for a long time.

8th Feeling a little better, not so sick.

9th Back to clinic for doctor visit and chemo. Admitted to hospital because of dehydration.

10th Received chemo by IV.

11th Home from hospital. Had treatment and given platelets before leaving. The nurse stuck your finger and it bled for about 1 hour.

12th Candy stayed up for a long time today. Played cards & computer.

13th Sunday. Little lazy today. Hair is getting loose.

14th Monday. Back to clinic for shot of chemo in leg. Hooked up IV.

15th Candy's big day for checkup. Sixth graders at school had special prayer request for you. School is waiting to hear report of checkup. Got good report, red blood cell count good, white count low. Had spinal bone marrow done with 5 types of chemo.

16th Candy had her aunt cut her hair because it was falling out so much. This week is critical to try for no fever.

19th Admitted back to hospital. (Not released from hospital until June 4th.)

20th Hospital moved Candy to bigger room 562.

22nd Another spinal done today.

24th Candy made the top 5 in GPA averages in whole 6th grade. Her picture was posted on the board in the main lobby of the school.

25th Noticed Candy was breaking out with bumps. Not sure what is cause.

26th Hospital started emergency IV medication for yeast infection.

27th White blood cells beginning to grow, up to 100.

28th Test results showed Candy to have a slow growing fungus or yeast infection called Candida in her blood stream. Candy was put in ICU. They wouldn't let Mom & Dad stay with you so they slept at end of hall by ICU waiting area. Candy said babies kept her awake all night. EKG showed no fungus inside stomach.

29th You had medicine for fungus through IV at 10:00. Candy real sick with fever & fast heartbeat 165-170, blood pressure 100/109. Brother Norman our pastor from New Life Baptist and another pastor from Cedar Grove Baptist came to visit. Candy was moved back to room 561. Chest X-ray done, chemo continued, white blood cells now 400.

30th Calvary Church will have prayer rally at 7:00 for Candy. Cat scan & bone scan done. Possible growth on the heart but good news: white cells still producing.

May 1997

1st Doctors from UAB Dept. of Forensic Science started strongest medicine hospital has for bacterial & yeast infection. Candy has bad rash and heart lesion found. Hole in her heart pumping the deadly Candida infection through her bloodstream. Doctors were expecting a bad night but you had a good one.

2nd White blood cells up to 6300. Platelets were up also.

3rd White blood cells up to 8200. I will never forget the look of hurtful dread shown on your Cousin Wendy's face when she saw you in ICU today. Candy got a new air bed to sleep on. Candy had an IV put in her groin area. Your mom & dad got real upset with hospital because they put the IV in while they had taken a quick break. Hospital said it was necessary to save Candy's life but Mom & Dad felt they should have been able to go in to hold you while IV was put in.

4th Candy got a feeding tube down her throat put in today. She was able to pull over on her right side all by herself.

5th Candy still in ICU. White cells & platelets still growing. Candy is trying to eat.

6th Bone scan was beautiful. Candy was moved out of ICU to room 575. She wanted a good night's sleep. She said the ICU was "too noisy."

7th Doctors doing chest & head scans on Candy today. Results clear.

8th Candy had a spinal tap today. It came back perfect. Candy taking antibiotics, got chemo in spine.

9th Not good news today. Fungus has affected your colon, liver & spleen. Candy played with her new

Game Boy. They cut her intake through her feeding down to 30cc.

10th Hospital stopped one of the antibiotics.

11th Mother's Day. Candy's fever was 103.

12th Candy passed some blood in stool. X-rayed stomach, scan found nothing. Stopped your food tube, began a different antibiotic & was given blood.

13th Still having some bleeding in her stool. Candy was able to stay awake more today.

14th Surgery today to put in live port under her arm. Left for surgery at 11:30 and returned 5:00 p.m.

15th Doctor did an ultrasound on heart. Leakage or hole in heart not as bad. Began using blower to help lungs that had collapsed. Principal from school came and gave Candy her Top 5 pin and certificate.

16th Feeding tube down your throat was removed today. It was what had caused internal bleeding from a cut it made when they pushed it down your throat.

18th Candy was given more blood today. She was able to stay awake longer.

20th They began therapy today with Candy. She got dressed like she was going to school.

21st Candy had to have fluids drawn out of her lungs today.

22nd Today Aunt Ann received your awards for you at school. You received 7 awards plus the top 5 pin. You asked the doctor when you could have a coke or coffee because you weren't allowed to drink anything.

23rd Candy's 12th birthday. Different shift nurses gave you two different birthday parties but you had to walk with a walker to parties. You were so sick. The children from school sent cards & gifts. You were a little fussy today but talked on the phone about your therapy.

24th Feeling better. Test results show no fungus in your lungs.

25th You played your new Game Boy. Your right foot & side have been hurting you today. We put your new therapy boots on you. You can now get up to use your bedsidepot. You took your pills & asked for unsweet tea.

27th You got a bath with rubber duckies today. You walked with your walker about 60 feet. Started you on a new chemo & doctors are saying you may be home in about one week.

28th Big Brother Jason's high school graduation is tonight. A paid ambulance trip was offered to take you to the graduation but you refused saying, "You didn't want to go unless you could walk in on your own."

29th Doctor found something in your brain scan. The fungus is now in your head & behind your eyes. Center for Infectious Disease came by to check on you.

30th Therapy today, you walked ten more feet. You are scheduled for a biopsy of a sore on your leg. Today Mom & Dad met with HUG center for training needed when you go home.

31st You had a good night but missing brother. He left for Florida on his graduation trip.

June 1997

1st Children's Miracle Network having a telethon in hospital. You got a WZZK t-shirt signed by Jim L, Dollar Bill & Patti from WZZK radio station. You said she didn't want to go on Channel 13 TV. You showed us where to go to get a blizzard ice cream. From 1:50 until 2:45 in your wheel chair you stayed downstairs in the lobby where all the excitement of the telethon was. You got more blood today. (300cc). Mom & Dad escaped to home for a short while to get your room ready for you to come home. Big Brother Jason called you from Florida. Nurses began putting steroids in your four-hour treatment that you have each day for your fungus infection that you have in your bloodstream. You have no fever.

2nd You were awake today for a biopsy taken on the inside of your little leg. Got 2 blue stitches. A special doctor came and gave you an eye exam. You have some fungus in your left eye but it has not affected your vision. Had hoped you could come home today but HUG center is not finished teaching Mom & Daddy how to work your lines and all your machines. You also had therapy today.

3rd Called your dad this morning. He said you had a good night. Had to get more blood today. HUG center met with Mom & Dad again to finish training.

4th You came home from hospital today.

5th Our God-sent nurse Ora Mae, who lives close by our house, came today and took a blood sample. She rushed back to hospital again because sample wasn't clear. You began eating some today.

6th Went back to clinic for checkup, things looking good. You had therapy today. Dad had to change your bandage over your central line today. He has to be so careful and use sterile rubber gloves. It has to be changed Monday, Wednesday & Fridays.

7th We can hold you up and walk you some & you are eating better.

10th Back to the clinic for a doctor checkup & a spinal tap.

11th Went back to clinic. You are being fed through your veins by a pump. Doctors made a change in the food that goes into your feeding bag.

13th Back in hospital for esophageal stricture. (You will be in hospital this time until July 4th.) Bubba has gone to Texas for a few days with some friends. You were able to lean upon your mom's shoulder today & she got you up by herself.

14th Mom so tired she slept for 3 ½ hours. You ate some chicken broth, but spitting up phlegm.

15th You are spitting up phlegm, can't take your medicine. You sat on hospital front porch for little while.

16th You couldn't eat or drink and having fever. Brother still in Texas. Your doctor is out of town for the week.

17th You were supposed to start back with your chemo but it again has been delayed. You are unable to swallow your medication. Tests were run and found you have a blockage in your throat. Your esophagus has closed up.

18th Heart scan done today and results good. Ran a biopsy on throat & waiting for results. Doctors think it is the Candida fungus infection in your throat.

19th Sent biopsy from throat to Texas from the Disease Control Center. Results: no fungus. Cat scan was also done and looked good.

20th You need more blood today. Infectious Disease doctors working to decide about medication since you can't take meds by mouth. Still in contact with Texas, waiting on decision from a special doctor about your central line.

21st Big brother Jason stayed with you so Mom & Dad could go home. You had therapy. Jason had you doing wheelies in your wheel chair down the hallway in front of nurses' station. You felt good today.

22nd Started your chemo up again at 9:00 p.m. & it will run for 24 hours. You are doing great, no fever with chemo. You drank some water and it stayed down, first time in a week. Feeling so good you let Daddy leave hospital and go to K-mart.

23rd Dad agreed for surgery to put a GT feeding button in your stomach. You are still on chemo. You spit up and it was green. The therapist took you to see two girls with GT feeding buttons. One was a white girl with lung problems & a black girl with intestine problems. She had a central line under her arm just like yours. You pushed and walked behind your wheelchair halfway & rode the other halfway. You had therapy 3 times today. Feeling good. Fever of only 99.6. They started you on some different chemo.

24th Finished your round of chemo that had run for 24 hours.

25th Surgery today, you had your GT installed in your stomach. (Mic-Key gastrostomy feeding tube). They came for you at 11:00 a.m. While in surgery, they also put in a string that goes from your mouth down your esophagus. This string was taped to the outside of your mouth. It will be used later to dilate your esophagus. Dr Cain called at 1:15 saying surgery was over & you are doing fine. Before they brought you back from recovery, there was trouble with the string. The opening was narrow. They finally brought you back to room at 2:00 p.m.

26th Today they got you up for therapy, no fever, you are doing fine.

27th You had therapy and sat in a chair for about 1 hour. You were given some pain medicine. You slept a lot.

28th Today you went for a lung x-ray, only the shadow that was seen before was there. Today you walked, sat up, brushed your teeth for 1st time, good job, from 1 hand to the other, you said it felt good. They put water in your tube. Waiting for Dr. Cain or Dr. Howard.

July 1997

1st You were scheduled to be put back asleep today. Doctor was going to use the string to dilate your esophagus. This didn't happen because your fever was 103.

2nd You are still running high fever.

3rd Still in hospital. Mom & Dad attending Hug Center: teaching how to prepare food bag.

4th You came home from the hospital. Platelet count 32,000.

5th You spit up blood about midnight.

6th Nosebleed, spit up blood & food about 5:30 p.m. Ora Mae, our nurse, came at 7:00 p.m., drew blood. Platelet count up to 55,000. Michael Crowe, our cousin & a newly ordained pastor, came by for prayer. You slept well & drank water. Throat burning, spit up big hunk of flesh about 11:00 p.m.

7th Slept good, drank water 2 times before 10:30. Feeling good. Called, left word for Dr. Cain who put your GT feeding button in.

8th Spinal tap today. Didn't need blood.

12th Put shoes & socks on by yourself; it took you 20 minutes because you insisted you needed no help that you could do it for yourself.

13th This time it only took 5 minutes for you to put on your shoes & socks. Doing foot & leg therapy.

14th Shoes & socks now only take 4 minutes. You did word puzzles 2 times. Your 1st day Civic Center to walk. You also played the piano. You wanted to try cabbage & corn beef; you took only 1 bite and didn't like it. You wanted chocolate milk and tea, drank it okay.

15th Back to hospital for more treatments.

16th Hospital still.

17th Came home from hospital.

20th Sick from chemo today.

21st You pulled up from your bed, holding to a chair for the first time, and then you cried because you were so happy & Daddy cried also. Then when big brother, Jason & his best friend, Trey came home you wanted to show them how you could pull yourself up.

23rd Back to hospital 1 day surgery to have another throat dilation & spinal tap.

28th Candy's baby cousin, Nikki, was born today. Candy felt like God had given her Nikki because she needed something little to hold in her arms & to love. Candy nicknames her new cousin "Mini Me."

August 1997

2nd Community of Odenville gave you Candy's Fun Day. You were able to attend. Everyone was so excited to see you. Channel 6 news there. There were all kinds of games, booths and tournaments for your benefit.

5th Back in hospital for more chemo--stayed in hospital until Aug. 9.

8th Put to sleep for throat dilation & another spinal with chemo.

9th Back home today but you were sick all day from the chemo and spinal.

11th Went to therapy.

12th Back to clinic for chemo. All counts good.

20th Back to hospital 1 day surgery put asleep for throat dilation & and another spinal.

21st Went home for a few days.

26th Admitted back in hospital for more chemo.

29th Got to go home.

September 1997

2nd back in hospital 1 day surgery, throat dilation. Good news, throat opening is larger, 28 out of 50.

5th Home but not feeling good.

10th Home but still sick, throwing up.

16th Admitted back in hospital for last round of chemo. Also another heart test done.

19th Got to go home but sick. You were nominated for Miss Homecoming court at school but you turned it down.

23rd You hurt your foot on your stair stepper trying to learn to walk again.

24th Went to clinic. Blood work good & foot x-ray ok.

27th Rode a bike outside for the 1st time.

October 1997

3rd Today is your brother Jason's 19th birthday. Went to clinic for fungus tests. You went and watched the homecoming parade in Odenville.

8th Back to 1 day surgery for another throat dilation and spinal and bone marrow tests. Good results. They put an IV in your groin area today at hospital and your mom was upset over that.

9th Today you walked on walker by yourself, then washed dishes and fixed your bubba a sandwich.

14th Went to therapy today.

16th Went to therapy today.

22nd Walked with your new leg braces today for 4 or 5 steps.

November 1997

December 1997

1st Spinal tap

10th Spinal tap

23rd You walked by yourself today, a miracle.

24th Christmas Eve. To clinic for blood work & chemo. (Weight 74 lbs, & height 59 ¾ inches)

January 1998

7th Clinic

8th Clinic

14th Clinic, Candy was sick today.

18th Candy's best friend, Sonya, 16 years old, from the hospital who was battling a different type of leukemia, died today at 1:15 p.m.

19th You were sick and throwing up and back was hurting.

20th Candy real bad off, rushed to hospital late tonight & put in ICU as critical, she actually died for 5 minutes & they had to shock her heart back to beating; she was put on life support ventilator. Given more blood.

23rd Still in ICU. They removed some of your tubes today from a machine.

24th Still in ICU. Today your back was red like a burn.

25th Still in ICU. Today you were red; it looked like you were burned from head to toe.

30th Still in ICU but today they took out your nose tube.

31st Still in ICU. You got a new IV put in your hand.

February 1998

1st Still in hospital but finally removed from ICU and back in a room

2nd-9th Still in hospital

10th Home but Candy can only have ice, nothing by mouth.

13th Back to clinic for doctor visit. Still can have only ice.

17th Back to clinic. Candy was able to start on clear liquids

20th Clinic again, Candy began eating food watching carbohydrates.

24th Back to Clinic.

27th Back to Clinic.

March 1998

3rd Clinic

Mary Ellen Sparks

4th Clinic

8th Candy ate barbeque

10th Clinic for spinal (only 3 or 4 more spinals to go)

13th Candy went to Wal-Mart

14th Candy went grocery shopping & pushed buggy

15th Candy rode 4-wheeler by herself

17th Clinic

18th Candy got sick during night

20th-22nd Back In hospital for chemo and spinal.

25th Clinic

April 1998

1st Clinic today for spinal and chemo & it was one year today she was diagnosed with leukemia

8th Clinic for checkup. Candy took cookies in for the doctors & nurses. No chemo today.

15th Clinic

22nd Clinic

29th Clinic

May 1998

5th Candy rode bicycle by herself 1st time today

6th Clinic

13th Clinic for spinal

20th One day surgery, removed Candy's central lines & her GT belly feeding button.

23rd Candy's 13th birthday

27th Clinic

28th Candy took a real bath for 1st time and was able to lie down in water.

30th Candy went swimming in Truett's pool

June 1998

9th Clinic

10th Clinic

17th Clinic

24th Clinic but no chemo today; Candy's liver functions were low. She is sick.

July 1998
1st Clinic
2nd Candy feeling bad today, her back hurts.
3rd Still feeling bad with back
7th Clinic
15th Clinic for spinal tap
21st Clinic

October 1998
5th Clinic for spinal

November 1998
30th Clinic for last spinal

Special note:
WBC, white blood count normal was 4.5-13.5 thous/MCL
RBC, red blood cell normal 4:00-5.20 thous/MCL
Platelet count normal was 140-440 thous/MCL)

Additional Stories of Faith

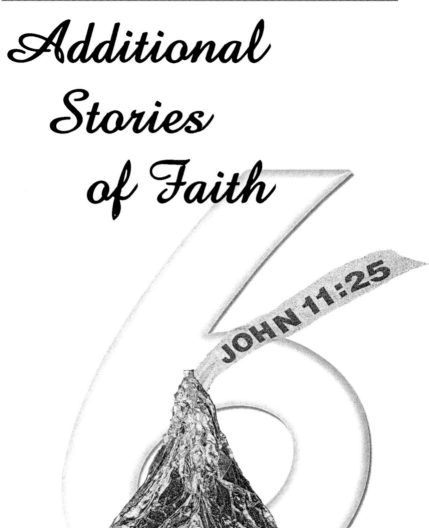

Here are some additional stories of faith that I would like to share with you.
—Mary Ellen Sparks

Thank you, Jesus, for choosing us to be Candy's and Jason's Mom & Dad and for finding us worthy to go on this incredible life changing journey. This is our love story.

The love of my life, my complete opposite

(A tiny bit of background before I continue: Our journey has taken us ahead to year 2011. Bobby and I are Destin bound, no kids, just the two of us. As we sit in Cracker Barrel and also as we continue on our drive to Destin, I'm looking back nostalgically.)

It's a beautiful toasty warm May morning. Car packed with deep sea fishing rods and reels, tackle box, ice chest, a couple pairs of shorts, tank tops and off we go, my hubby and me, en route to sunny Destin, Florida. Excitement fills the air. Stopping at the Cracker Barrel for an early morning breakfast before our long drive, I laugh as I wonder how two people so completely different can be so perfect together. I smile as I look down at our plates. My eggs fried so hard they could bounce off the wall; his seem uncooked with the yellow running. I have milk, he chooses coffee. I have grits, he has potato casserole. I have bacon, he has ham. My pancakes are loaded with syrup, his have blue berries. I get toast, he gets biscuits.

As I sit here in the Cracker Barrel looking out at the window, my mind races back to a younger time in my very own life, a time when I first met Bobby: It was July 4th weekend 1971. I was 19. Kim, my best friend, and I had decided on the spur of the moment to take a first time trip to Florida. I sold my car tape player to my younger brother, Chuck, to get enough money to go. No reservations made, we took off for the unknown. Going for the gusto was so out of character for me. I couldn't believe that my mom and dad even let me go. Kim and I literally walked the streets of Panama City Beach, Florida all day begging for someone to allow us to rent a cheap motel room. None was available, everyone booked solid. Soaking up the hot sun and enjoying the rolling waves, we sat on our multicolored beach blanket enjoying all the excitement all around us. The beach was full of people, all laughing and having fun. Suddenly five good looking fellows walked in front of us, so macho and carefree. One guy with jet black hair, sky blue eyes, cut off jeans, no shirt and gorgeous broad shoulders caught my eye. I turned to my friend, Kim and playfully said, "I like it, I like it, I want it, I want it." We both giggled, mostly because that was extremely out of character for little ole sly protected me, weighing only 90 pounds. I had long straight brown hair kind of like Cher. Kim was sexier, always more courageous and aggressive than I. She had always gotten first choice of any of the guys we met. I was surprised when two of the five hunks came back our way. I was totally caught off guard when the gorgeous one with the most beautiful shoulders I had ever seen chose me over Kim. I never believed in love at first sight but the feeling inside me was warm and trembling and like nothing I had felt before. When I looked into his beautiful sky blue eyes, I felt I was enveloped in the most unique and different feeling. It seemed to radiate all through my body.

Talk about being bent out of shape. Kim had never been rejected before. She wanted to be with Bobby. It was not supposed to be like this. She was his type, not me. After about thirty minutes of talking and flirting, Bobby, for some unknown reason, stood up, got a cold beer, popped it opened and proceeded to pour it over my head. It was his beer. Kim and I were not drinking. As the cold beer ran down my face I hated him. I never wanted to see him again in my entire lifetime. The nerve of him! Kim and I didn't even have a motel room. We didn't know where we would sleep that night. Where in the world would I be able to go to change clothes? I was so mad. Bobby laughed as he wrestled me to the ground. He was so big and strong. With his arms around my little 19 1/2 inch waist, I fought for all I was worth. Suddenly his lips were on mine. I'll never forget it as long as I live. That exact moment that he kissed me a little old man and his wife walked by our blanket. I looked up to see the old couple holding hands. With a smile lighting up her face the old lady said, "**Oh, to be young and in love again.**" That phrase of hers seemed to float in mid-air. Like the song that goes, "*That kiss, that wonderful kiss.*" I couldn't fight Bobby off anymore and I thought to myself, *my mama would be so disappointed in me.* My body went limp and I felt myself melt into Bobby's strong arms and I have been there ever since.

Suddenly, I snap back into reality as I hear my hubby, Bobby say, "Mary Ellen, Mary Ellen, you need to finish your breakfast! Those big red snappers in Destin await us. We're going to be late. Hurry up, we got to get going." As we parade out the door from Cracker Barrel, Destin bound, I said a prayer of thanks. Bobby decides he will drive for a while so I snuggle up with my blanket and small pillow and stare out the car window. I'm so excited about going back to Destin.

*Suddenly, as if watching a movie of my life unfold, my mind **again** wants to daydream. I reminisce to the year 2000. Candy was 15 and Jason 21.*

I chuckle to myself as I remember that wonderful summer in sunny Destin, Florida. Candy had just turned 15 and after being sick for so long it was her dream to go back and stay at the Ramada Inn. Best friends Tabatha and Candice went with us. The girls had their own motel room which opened up right over the pool. They could literally walk out of their room and jump right into the pool. At 15, they loved to flirt with the guys swimming by their room. How much fun we had on that trip with Candy and those girls! Later that night, the girls had stayed by the pool so Candy and I went, just the two of us, for our midnight stroll on the beach. We were walking close to the water's edge and feeling the warm wet sand tickle our toes when playful laughter caught our attention. We both turned to see a teenage couple lying on a blanket next to the rolling white cap waves. We watched the couple. The strong muscular young guy was laughing out loud as he held the small delicate girl down, kissing her playfully.

Talk about a ***moment of Déjà vu'***, it felt like I was viewing a scene from my very own life. As we watched, the girl stopped fighting and melted into the big guy's arms. I had the strangest sensation; it felt like I had been here before, only before the roles were reversed. Then I had been the young girl on the blanket squirming and wrestling the big guy, and now I was the old lady walking by. I felt the hate again at Bobby for pouring that cold beer over my head but also I felt the loving warmth of his strong embrace and the taste of his hot lips on mine. Candy and I looked at each other with the same thought going through our heads. Candy giggled, "Mom, go ahead and do it, I know what you are thinking, just go ahead and say it. Do it Mom, come on, just do it!"

Candy giggled uncontrollably. Suddenly, I was the old woman looking down on that playful young couple and I knew they were in love even if they didn't realize it yet. So with hot tears flowing down my cheeks, tears of happiness and of happily of ever after, I said it, ***"Oh, to be young and in love again."*** I watched as my life came full circle.

Summary: They say opposites attract--all part of God's plan

God made Bobby and me so different. I'm very compassionate; I hurt when someone else hurts. Bobby is tougher and more tuned in to the real world than I am. I see the good in everyone and everything. Bobby always seems negative. Only recently, after 35 years of marriage, have I discovered that God gave Bobby a very special gift of being able to see things that other people can't see and feel things that other people aren't allowed to feel. I can't tell you how many times he has predicted situations would turn out a certain way and I at the same time would declare he didn't know what he was talking about. I see things through rose-colored glasses and he sees things in reality as they are. Our weaknesses and strengths are opposites. We enhance each other. Believe it or not, his weakness of being negative is really a great gift from God. Bobby doesn't realize it but he's tuned into God more than he knows and he always had been.

God always keeps him in touch with reality and the real world and it balances with the special gift God has given me of being compassionate and trusting. Bobby sees, feels, hears, tastes, and even smells things totally opposite from what I do. I finally realize how boring and one-sided this life would be if we were not created totally opposites. God revealed to me that through his illuminated plan I have the blessing of being able to see, feel, hear, taste and smell things two different ways at the same time. I see the world through my eyes and through Bobby's at the same time. Only God could create such a perfect thing known as love. I just realized how boring life would be if God hadn't made the *LOVE of My LIFE* so different from me. I often remind Bobby that our falling in love was destiny. He laughs and his sky blue eyes sparkle as he corrects me, **"No, Mary Ellen, It wasn't destiny, it was Panama City."**

At the end of the journey, when you see rainbows and breathtaking sunsets on the water, you can thank God but in the middle of the journey all you can do is trust God. Bobby and I have learned that, at the end of a journey like ours, God pours out his blessings on you and your family. So if you are going through tribulation and heartbreaking trials like we did, expect a shower of blessings at the rainbow's end.

Twenty-four hours a day God is there, backing me up, guiding me forward, ready to speak to me and always ready to listen. This chapter of my journey I refer to as:

Answers to Prayers

These stories of faith I have tucked warmly in my cathedral of memories for me to revisit many times as the years race by.

Flat tire, I saw Jesus wink at me

After all the ruckus and excitement of a fun-filled week long vacation in Destin, it was time to head home. I needed one last time to feel the warm ocean breeze on my face and smell the salty sea air. I took a quick stroll behind the condo to the beach before boarding the car. I embraced my surroundings with awe and wonder. I shut my eyes, wanting to memorize every detail. How I wished I could put it all in an envelope and stuff it in my pocket to reopen every day.

As I always do before getting in a car, I said my favorite silent prayer. "Please, Dear Jesus, stay close to me and my family, go before us and prepare the way for us, and be sure to be there when we get there." That simple prayer has worked wonders for me. It's what I call my "Go, no stay prayer." I like the feeling of knowing Jesus is beside me and, at the same time, I picture him going ahead of me and preparing the way and knowing that he will be there at my destination smiling waiting for me. All this he does without ever leaving the front seat next to us. Incredible yes, but totally do-able for Jesus.

After a short pit stop we headed back onto the interstate. I noticed that the interstate was extremely busy this particular day. Cars and eighteen-wheelers seemed to be cruising past us at very high speeds. Cars were maneuvering in and out of traffic passing each other. It reminded me of the Talladega 500. Everyone owned the road and didn't appear to care about anyone who got in their way. I thought to myself, *it's a wonder I don't see a bad wreck.*

A car appeared beside of us, slowed down to our speed and then I noticed a man with his window rolled down shouting at us. At first I thought, how rude. Then I realized he was trying to signal us to get off the road. He pointed to the tire, then shouted "Mister, you need to pull off the road now!" We reduced our speed and pulled off to the shoulder of the highway. To my horror, the mystery driver also pulled off the road and came to a stop several car lengths in front of us. As Bobby started to get out of the car to see what was happening, the mystery driver opened his passenger's side door and began running back in our direction. I said, "I don't like the look of this. It scares me. Why is he running back to us? What if it's a trick?" As Bobby jumped out, I heard him say, "Oh, he's just stopping to help us." Still I felt a cold chill go up my spine.

When all was said and done, the mystery driver turned out to be a special blessing or what I'd like to consider my special angel sent from God to keep us from a serious blowout that could have been deadly. What are the chances of this? The mystery driver didn't realize he knew us. He had only seen a car in serious danger of a blown out tire and something clicked inside of him saying, *you won't be able to live with yourself if you don't let that person know of the danger.* It turned out to be Mickey. He and our son, Jason, were close friends and had worked together. Many times in the past, Mickey had sat down at our supper table with us for a country home cooked meal.

I loved the times he had joined us because he always bragged on my cooking.

Now here he was coming to our rescue. He was traveling home after being on vacation in Gulf Shores. We were coming back from Destin. Hundreds and hundreds of cars passing us on the interstate and at the exact moment we needed help, Mickey appears from nowhere. No way something like that could have happened. What are the odds of that happening? Mickey's response was, "Isn't God great?" The total timing still amazes me, right when we needed help. I don't believe in coincidence. I believe in God, a very awesome God.

Gobel Mann, the bar stool and the grandbaby I knew I'd get someday.

Standing in my outdated kitchen, I felt as if I had been stuck in the 1960s Happy Days era.

All around me green. Old green metal cabinets, green refrigerator, green stove, even a green washer and dryer set. I expected Fonzie to walk through the back door giving me a thumbs up proclaiming, "Aaaayyyy.......Mrs. C." How I longed for a new modern kitchen. I shut my eyes for a minute to visualize the beautiful light oak wooden cabinets. I felt a warm feeling envelop me as I imagined my gorgeous new walls and cabinets, laughter floating through the air as we share a family dinner in our new kitchen.

That's it. I made up my mind. I'm going to remodel my kitchen. It all sounded so easy until my logical thinking hubby reminded me of all the many decisions we would need to make and how we would need to measure for everything and think things out before we went wild. So many choices and so much expertise needed. "Several major stores around have model kitchens to view. That's a good place to get some ideas," my hubby said. With that he added, "Counter tops will be a separate issue. Don't forget your sink, dishwasher and new refrigerator; you'll need to hire a plumber." He handed me tape measure. "Correct measurements are very important." I had a knack for believing everything would magically fall into place but he knew better.

I proclaimed, "I can do this. You just wait and see." He winked at me as he left the kitchen. I turned to notice he was grinning from ear to ear and laughing under his breath. He thought all this was so funny. He knew I didn't have a clue how to begin.

I went from store to store. The more model kitchens I visited, the more distressed I became. I felt overwhelmed with all the choices and decisions. To myself I thought, *I need someone with a lot of expertise but who do I trust?* I heard a voice loud and clear in my head, "Trust me." I felt like that old TV juice commercial where you see someone thump their fingers to their head and say, "Dah, I could've had a V8."

Why hadn't I thought of this before? I knew from past adventures that when I make the decisions on my own, everything always ends up in a big mess. I get too deep in things and nothing seems to fall into place. **One thing so wonderful about faith is that you don't have to figure out how to make it happen** and you don't have to figure out all the nitty gritty details. Just trust God and watch him unfold the answer before your eyes. He works in ways that you and I could never think of. I turned my dilemma over to Jesus, asking him to get me to the right person, and at the right price, real cheap.

The next weekend, my sister-n-law, Mary Ann, and I had a yard sale. Just so happened an elderly man and his wife drove up in a fairly new pickup truck. I noticed he was tall, slender and attractive, walked a little straight-legged with a slight limp. He walked with the grace of a straight and tall cowboy. Things just clicked when my sister-n-law introduced me to Mr. Gobel Mann, a cabinet maker from Margaret, Alabama. A light bulb went off in my head as I immediately knew this was the answer to my prayer. I told Mr. Mann of my dilemma. I loved to hear him talk. He said, "Sure, Honey, I can do it for you. That is if you are not in a real big hurry. You see I'm 82 years old and rest when I get tired." His eyes were shining as if they had little flashlights behind them. With his tape measure and small notepad and pencil in hand, we walked though our pasture to my kitchen to take measurements. *Thank you, Dear Jesus,* I said to myself.

A few days later, I visited Mr. Mann's workshop behind his house. I was amazed at his handiwork. His workshop displayed walls full of cabinets, all sizes and styles. What craftsmanship. The major store's model kitchens were plain and dull compared to his divine skillful work. I found Mr. Gobel Mann to be a true Christian and someone I could totally trust. He said, "At my age I don't need any money. I've got all the money I need so I'm going to give you a good price." He ordered special blue custom made counter tops and sized them to fit around my new sink and dishwasher. He didn't make a penny off those countertops. He gave them to me at his cost. He designed a shelf underneath my cabinet for my new microwave. Mr. Gobel Mann touched my life. A World War II hero, he was injured when a piece of metal lodged in the side of his head. He couldn't read nor write yet he had a God-given gift of cabinetry. He loved people, treated them fairly and talked a lot about Jesus and heaven.

It took a long time to complete my kitchen but how I enjoyed going over to his house and watching my new cabinets come to life in his workshop. He had to stop every so often and go in the house and lie down with oxygen because breathing wood dust would get to him. His little wife always had something cooking that smelled so delightful. Gobel Mann's eyes twinkled as he shared with me his love stories of coming home from the war to his little wife who truly was the love of his life.

Gobel Mann designed and created the most beautiful light oak kitchen cabinets you ever laid your eyes on. I love my new wall to ceiling huge white pantry and wall to wall cabinets over my new washer and dryer set in my utility room. He and his son, Bill, even did the installation for me. One last special request I made to Mr. Gobel Mann. I asked him to design me a small bar with only one high-backed stool and I wanted it at the end of my cabinets. Candy said, "That little bar will be mine to eat and play on." In anticipation I added, "And one day my little grandson will claim this to be his very own. He will sit on that high stool close to me while I wash dishes and cook." Oh, I didn't have a grandson yet but I knew someday I would have one.

Years later I ran into Mr. Gobel Mann. He had lost his little wife. She made it to heaven before him. "I'm 87 now," he said with laugher to his voice. The piece of metal in his head from World War II had shifted. He went blind and had surgery that restored his sight. After all these many years the government was finally helping him because of his war injury and his eyes danced as he said, "I'm getting a purple heart." He also said, "If God had made me a preacher instead of a cabinet maker I would have had two buckets outside the church doors. I'd tell people to give to God in one bucket and if there is a little tiny bit left over you can put a dab in my bucket. You know something; I'm convinced that both buckets would be overflowing. That's the way God works."

God answered my prayer for the perfect person to design and create my new kitchen and utility room, and at the perfect price, real cheap. I thank God for Mr. Gobel Mann.

By the way, I got my little grandson that I wanted so very much. Cody Dallas sits in that high backed stool under my little bar that Mr. Gobel Mann designed for me out of love.

Do all the good you can, in all the ways you can, for all the people you can, while you can.

Angels working overtime

I could write a book about the many occasions that angels have literally jumped to our rescue to prevent me and my family from dangers. A few months ago, Candy's brother, Jason, was traveling in his big Ford truck. A huge dead tree actually fell from the side of the highway and literally came crushing through his windshield and dash. My son had felt the tremendous force and thought at first that a low flying plane had actually crashed and hit his truck. Thank God, my son had an incredible urge to duck down in the seat while keeping total control of his vehicle. Upon impact the tree came through the windshield and broke through the dash. Mr. Beard, a guy that works for Jason, was in the back seat when the event happened and he watched in horror as the tree jammed its way through the window and left a big huge hole in the windshield right in front of where Jason was sitting. He couldn't see Jason and his first fear was that Jason's head had been cut off. He said he couldn't bear to look until he heard Jason speak up. Jason had miraculously ducked way down to the floor board just in time to avoid the tree. The whole tremendous tree came to a landing lodged in between Jason and his nephew, Justin, who was also in the front seat. All three guys came out of this horrifying event unhurt but shaken up. You would wonder how the three guys survived after seeing the pictures of Jason's truck. The tree and the damage were massive. I told Jason he had worked his angels overtime and that all three of them should get down on their knees that night and thank God because it could have turned out a lot different. That thought made me shudder.

God hears a mother's prayers. Many times each day and even during the night I say my special prayer asking God to send angels to watch over me and my family. When Jason called to tell me of the tree coming through the windshield and dash, I knew how important angels are in protecting us.

I have one other thing to share with you about a recent car wreck Candy, our 85-year-old Aunt Lucy and I had. Candy was driving. Aunt Lucy sat in the passenger seat and I was in the backseat behind Candy. We were horrified when a driver going the opposite direction lost control of his vehicle on the highway and was heading straight toward us. Candy's fast thinking saved our lives as she dodged his out-of-control vehicle and headed off the side of the road. We were almost out of harm's way when the out-of-control car hit our rear-end fender causing us to go airborne. Unfortunately, there was a huge embankment that we went down. Our Chevy Blazer flipped over three times before coming to a landing with all four wheels removed, all windows broken out and a complete drive shaft thrown ten feet away from our vehicle. I literally felt the angels' arms holding all three of us inside the vehicle. I was the only one hurt because, from the back seat while our car was flipping over, I tried desperately to reach Candy in the front seat; not that I could have done anything to help her, but my instincts were to try to reach her. We were told later by the driver of the car that hit us that he had a tire blow out and he had lost complete control of his vehicle. He was very sorry but what is remarkable is that he told us he had seen a gas main line and his car was heading straight toward it. He couldn't control the car at all and he thought he had hit the gas main line because his air bag exploded and his car filled up with smoke. He had lots of trouble getting out of his car. His vehicle clipped the end of our fender causing us to flip our Blazer over an embankment but the impact of the wreck broke his distance to the gas main line and thus kept him alive.

Candy in 2008

He would have died had he hit that main gas line. In fact, when the smoke appeared from the air bag he said he thought he had in fact hit the gas line and that he was dying. It's safe to say he had angels watching over him that day also. Totally awesome! Don't you agree?

To see the pictures from our completely totaled out vehicle you would wonder how Candy, Aunt Lucy and I survived. Aunt Lucy being in her eighties was sore but uninjured. The driver side of the car was crushed in so much that we couldn't open the doors from that side. We had to push the passenger side doors with our feet to exit the vehicle. Of course, by that time many other cars had stopped and there were all kinds of people running to our rescue. Candy told me later that as our Blazer was flipping over and over she thought she was dying. It was a terrible feeling that seemed to last forever but actually was over really quick. This wasn't funny then but now all three of us can laugh about it. The last thing Candy remembered before we flipped was hearing her mom shout out "O God, O God" and at the same time hearing our 85-year-old Aunt Lucy shout out "Oh, Sh_ _!"

Jesus has a sense of humor

Let me tell you that Jesus has a sense of humor. Sometimes I can almost hear him laughing and I visualize that radiant smile of his as he chuckles. I imagine how his eyes shine like they have little flashlights in them.

Has this ever happened to you? You misplaced something that you just had in your hands. You think to yourself, *"It has to be here somewhere. I just had it. Dummy me, what could I have done with it*?" You look through all the piles around you over and over but to no avail, you still can't find what you just had. Or has this happened to you? You put something away in a safe place so you will know exactly where it is when you need it. Now the time is here. You need that item. Why can't you remember where you put it?

Try this. I have to do this all the time. I confess to Jesus, *"I'm so glad, Jesus, that you are all wise and all knowing. I'm so scattered-brain and forgetful. I'm so thankful that you know everything. Please help me find this item I need to find right now. I love you, Dear Jesus. Thank you."* You will be amazed how Jesus will simply uncover that item for you. Because it is important to you, it is important to Jesus.

He shaved his head to match Candy's

As I look at the cozy little church nestled between colorful yellow, brown, red and orange rolling mountains, I feel God's presence so strong. This is where my son Jason and his fiancée Jennifer will be married in a few weeks. Beside the church sits an old cemetery, well kept with big headstones, all adorned with beautiful flowers and some lined with small angel statues. Jennifer's precious little mother is buried here.

Overlooking the top of the cemetery you see a big statue of Jesus, his arms outstretched in love. Behind

Candy's personality

him stand three wooden crosses. As I walk inside the church my breath seems to be caught in my throat as I stand in awe. What a feeling inside this small wooden church with a total of eighteen pews. As Mr. Venable opens the church doors for us, I reminisce of Brandon, his grandson. Brandon and Candy's brother, Jason, were best friends during high school. I had past visions of Candy being so sick and remembering how she would sit for hours with Brandon on a small bench playing video games. Their arms wrapped around each other's neck. You could hear laughter and challenges throughout the whole house. Brandon shaved his head to match Candy's almost bald head. She would never wear a hat. Two bald heads sitting next to each other. What a sight. Candy had lost her ability to walk so when she needed to move to another room Brandon would sweep her up in his strong arms with her little arms wrapped around his neck and he would carry her to the next room. She always kissed him on the cheek as he sat her down. Now that's love in motion.

Candy in 2011

Epilogue

Candy's treatments lasted over three years and her follow-up blood tests took us through a total of 10 years. I remember early in her treatment while at Children's Hospital, Candy was getting ready to receive more much needed blood when I met a young mother whose little boy would need a blood transfusion every month for the rest of his life just to keep him alive. The young mother said something to me about her little boy that I thought was so strange. "Jesus loves him more than I do." I wondered, *"How could a mother ever say such a thing? I loved my Candy so very much and I could not imagine anyone being able to love her more than I did."*

I also remember a preacher who came to visit us at the hospital saying, "Good will come out this." To myself, I thought, *"How can good come out of anything so bad?"* As the years rolled by I realized that Jesus has a soft spot for Moms. Loud and clear he hears their pleas and prayers for their children. How comforting it is to know that Jesus does indeed love our children far more than we love them and that good does come from terrible heartbreaking trials and tribulations.

If you were to ask me how we knew that Candy would live, marry and become a mother herself one day I'd have to say, "God said it, we believe it and that settles it." So as the years continue to pass by I have the total assurance that it's going to happen. If someone asks will Candy be able to have children I can answer, absolutely. Here's why:

My brother Tom (Candy's Uncle Bud) is also a miracle from God. He's alive today only because of a liver transplant that came through for him the Friday after Thanksgiving Day way back when Candy was so sick. Because we had been through such trauma with Candy, my family had chosen not to tell us that Bud was real sick and in need of a liver transplant to survive. My Christian neighbor, Mrs. Hall, had been the one to break the news to me accidently when she asked about my brother. Mrs. Hall's daughter was part of Bud's church family. So on that Friday after Thanksgiving I was there when my brother came out of recovery. While we were so thankful for his transplant, our hearts ached for the family of the one who had donated that liver. Bud, wide-awake, very emotional, held his hand up to motion for me to come by his side. He couldn't wait to tell me that while he was under anesthesia Jesus revealed to him that Candy would be healed, marry and have a child. He was totally sure of what had been revealed to him concerning Candy's future. We kid Bud about him getting an evangelistic liver because he woke up praising the Lord. The Doctors had once told us that Candy may not be able to have children but through the years as she was healed I was able to tell her with total confidence that I know for sure that she will have at least one child. Bud wasn't told how many children, only that Candy would indeed be healed, marry and have a child. God said it; we believe it and it's all settled.

Also concerning Candy's future, this happened to me. Fast forward ahead three years after Bud was given his vision about Candy I, too, was told something spectacular. This also happened on a Friday after Thanksgiving. I remember the day well because Candy and two of her close girlfriends, Candice and Tabatha and I had spent Thanksgiving night at a hotel that adjoined a huge indoor mall so we could be first in line for all the after-Thanksgiving sales. Candy was fifteen and was just beginning to get her life back together. Walking was still a little difficult for her at that point. God gave me a thirty-second glimpse of the one who would one day be Candy's husband.

I heard the words loud and clear, *Candy's husband.* I ran back in the store with the intent of memorizing every single detail of his boy who would one day be the man Candy would marry. I wanted to be able to recognize him in the future when he came into our lives but that wasn't God's intent. I looked everywhere but the one I was looking for wasn't anywhere to be found. God gave me that whispered knowledge only to ease my mind to let me know he has someone very special in store for Candy. He wanted me to know that Candy would be healed, marry and eventually have children. There were several things that I did remember from that thirty-second encounter and I quickly embedded those details in my mind, including the big smile he had thrown to Candy and the big smile she had thrown back his way. All through Candy's growing up years I was able to tell her with confidence, "You just wait and see what God has in store for you." God said it; I believe it and that settles it for me.

Fourteen years have come and gone.
What we went through hurt so bad and seemed never ending. We felt so helpless but never alone. We stand so humble in thanking God for all the many caring people he placed directly in our path to help

us physically, emotionally and financially. All the prayers from believers that went up to heaven on our behalf were incredible. It was love overflowing and outpouring on us in our time of need. Now at the end of that journey we see beauty where we never saw it before; colorful rainbows, stunning sunrises, breathtaking sunsets and butterfly effect memories all around us. To me, sunsets are God's magnificent signature at the end of each day.

My family and friends were always asking when my book would be completed. The timing just didn't feel right. Our emotions were still too raw and painful to recall. Candy's healing took a long time and also healing had to come for Mom, Dad and brother Jason. It was a long difficult road. This past summer I started getting nudges from God telling me he wanted this story finished now. That old devil didn't want this book to be out here. There was a time when he got my family down, rock bottom down. He jumped on us, kicked us and tried to keep us down. It hurt so badly but, with all of that, our faith has increased. What is inside of me, Bobby, Jason and Candy is far greater than what is inside that old devil. He can't do to us what he did before. As he tries, we throw the book at him, the Word of God, the Bible. We have learned that whatever situation you are facing, God's Word has the answer. When I started writing this book this time with the intent of finishing it, I got really ill. I started having severe vertigo attacks. There were three episodes that included bright lights flashing all around my head, extreme spinning and tossing so violent that it felt that someone picked me up and was trying to throw me across the room. It felt like there was no floor underneath me. I thought I was dying. The hospital thought I was having a stroke or aneurysm. Thank God it wasn't either. Each time I would try to work on my book, I just couldn't think or focus. That went on for a couple of months. I have learned to hold on to God's hand and his word so I got all that behind me. Then just as my book was about to be completed, my desktop computer fried. Now as I finish the last of my book, my laptop computer is shutting off every fifteen minutes. I told Bobby, "That old devil doesn't want this book out there, but God does."

I have one last thought to leave you with. These few words are worthy of being taped to your bathroom mirror or carried inside your wallet. Many times, I remind Candy of these thoughts as she goes through all the new adventures in her life. It's my prayer that

Candy's Graduation Day

these words will help you in whatever chapter of your own life you are going through right now.

1) The devil is not all wise and all knowing.

2) The devil cannot be at all places at the same time.

3) The devil cannot read your mind.

Only God can do these things. God is in total control. His love, mercy and salvation are never ending and immeasurable. God is omniscient and omnipotent.

If Satan keeps reminding you of your past, try reminding him of his future.

Final note:

There is a young handsome lawyer hanging out at our house these days keeping Candy happy. I love hearing her laugh and seeing that cute little dimple brighten up her smile. I think she is in love. I got tickled the other day when I heard the young handsome lawyer say, "Candy isn't right, but she's just right for me." Candy has one cute dimple and the young handsome lawyer has two. (I think God threw the dimples in as an added bonus.) Maybe it's time I began praying asking God to give me another grandbaby in a few years, this one with cute dimples.

Thank you for going on this journey with us.

We hope you find the miracle in your life that you need. God bless you much.

Candy wrote this when she was in Mrs. Sewell's 1st grade class. Now Candy is living out her dream of being a teacher. She teaches 4th grade.

Candy today

Today, my miracle, Candy Kisses, is 26 years old, beautiful, petite, dainty, healthy and extremely happy and still brightening the lives of everyone around her. Her cute little dimple is still shining. I have heard her say that she wouldn't change anything from her past because those experiences shaped her future and made her into the person she is today. She graduated with a Bachelor's of Social Work degree and a Minor in Criminal Justice for Juveniles and then went on to earn her Master's of Early Childhood and Elementary Education. While attending UAB she was President of Phi Alpha Honor Society. Now she is living out her dream of being a school teacher. (Mom still visualizes her as a little girl; always playing school,

Candy today

writing lessons on her big huge chalk board that extended the entire width of one of her bedroom walls.) Candy teaches 4th grade and most of her students are bigger than she is. Candy cherishes life and loves all of her kids. She says, "How awesome it feels to walk down the halls of the same school I once attended myself and now be a teacher."

Even away from school, children are Candy's life. She is the Children's Ministry Director at Calvary Baptist Church and in addition to that she teaches kindergarten through 5th grade during Sunday School and Extended Sessions. She often chaperones the teens on trips. Some of Candy's kids still call her **Ms. Candy** from her church ministry and prior daycare teaching and some call her **Ms. Sparks** from her new

Candy and her brother, Jason

role as 4ᵗʰ grade teacher. Candy never misses a chance to say, ***"I love you"***. Thank God Candy is considered cured now. The only remaining problem Candy has is taking insulin shots as a result of the pancreatitis that caused her cardiac arrest that horrible night. Mom still tells everyone, "If you want to see how good God is, look at my Candy."

Big Bubba Jason today

To update you on Candy's big brother Jason, he and Jennifer are married. She is my beautiful daughter-in-law and an outstanding mother. I don't know if I could have ever known true happiness without having a son. Jason holds my heart. He's the light of my life. I love him so very much. Jason is the owner of River Oaks Landscaping Solutions and Tree Removal Services. As you might guess Jason is now one terrific dad. My two grandchildren he has given me are exactly the same age difference that Jason and Candy were so it's like having them all over again. Jason's son looks and acts like a mini Jason. The little fellow wants to be just like his dad. His baby sister calls him her Bubba. He once told me that he will not answer or even look at his baby sister unless she calls him Bubba. He holds her close when she is hurt or sick just like his daddy always held his baby sister Candy when she was hurt or sick. That's what big Bubbas are for.

Author Mary Ellen Sparks

About the Author:

Mary Ellen Sparks and her husband Bobby are still in love and now retired. She enjoys fishing and spending time with their two young grandchildren. Mary Ellen loves seeing the fiery orange sunset, especially on the water. Colors are more intense for her now and she sees beauty where she never saw it before.

Mary Ellen's sister is also an author. In her new book, among many other colorful characters, her sister, Judy, will introduce you to their Great Grandfather, Rev. Tom Sexton, The Blacksmith Preacher.

Mary Ellen likes to refer to her Great Grandfather as the Billy Graham of the horse and buggy era.

He was a staggering drunk who was transformed into a powerful instrument for God.

Rev. Tom Sexton shared the pulpit with Billy Sunday, R.A. Torrey, and other well-known preachers. He had a very unusual way of praying by just stopping where he was at, looking up and talking out loud directly to God. His prayers were not eloquent but God answered him in mighty ways. My Great Grandfather, Rev. Tom Sexton, preached in 26 states and saved over 30,000 people. One other thought worth mentioning, the famous Rev. Tom Sexton was born on April 1, 1858.

Candy was diagnosed with leukemia on April 1, 1997. April Fools Day, how ironic.

Hope you will read Judy's new exciting book, *Tennessee Valley Echoes, Tales And Memories That Refuse To Die*, by Judith Biddle.

Special Thanks to:

Dr. Roger Berkow, M.D. and all the doctors and nurses from Children's Hospital of Birmingham

Ora Mae Layton, RN

Magic Moments for granting Candy's wish of the Jacuzzi Whirlpool Hot Tub

Peggy Hughes, Cathy Kelley, Brother Norman LeCroy, Mary Ann Hardy, Michael Crowe, Evelyn Johnson

TV Anchor Andrea Lindenburg, St. Clair News-Aegis

Rick & Bubba 104.7 radio show FM

Uncle Clifford Sparks for always tickling Candy's feet while she was in the hospital.

Robert, Scarlet and Brandon Terrell for giving us our special gift of Sonya, now up in heaven.

All our family, friends, co-workers and neighbors who lovingly carried us on their shoulders through this journey. We pray God will bless you all. We couldn't have made it without you.

TO GOD BE THE GLORY

Thank you, Mr. Gabriel
I would like to thank my publisher, Mr. Gabriel Vaughn (whom I fondly call Mr. Gabriel), at Legacy Book Publishing for his expertise in creating my cover and publishing my book.

I love his Archangel name and I love this verse.

And the angel answering said unto him, I am Gabriel, that stand in the presence of God: and am sent to speak unto thee, and to shew thee these glad tidings.

Luke 1:19 AKJV

Check out his website at:

www.LegacyBookPublishing.com